What
Would

Audrey

Do?

Timeless Lessons for
Living with Grace and Style

What
Would

Audrey

Do?

PAMELA KEOGH

Aurum
Press

First Published in Great Britain 2008
by Aurum Press Ltd, 74-77 White Lion Street, London N1 9PF
www.aurumpress.co.uk

This paperback edition first published in 2015 by Aurum Press Ltd

Published by arrangement with Gotham Books, a division of Penguin
Group (USA) Inc.

A catalogue record for this book is available from the British Library.

ISBN 978 1 78131 465 4

2019 2018 2017 2016 2015
10 9 8 7 6 5 4 3 2 1

Designed by Sabrina Bowers
Illustrations by Monika Roe
Printed in China

| For Linda Chester |

Contents

Introduction   1

1. Audrey as Movie Star   11

2. Romance Central   37

3. Zen Audrey   67

4. Home Studies   87

5. On the Road   115

6. "A Very Stylish Girl . . ."   131

7. Heartbreak and Solace   165

8. Modern Times   181

9. St. Audrey   205

10. Legend   223

Acknowledgments   251

Index   255

Introduction

Audrey Hepburn came to the attention of most Americans in September 1953, when she got above-the-title billing as Princess Ann in *Roman Holiday*—capturing the heart of her costar, Gregory Peck, as well as a generation of moviegoers who wondered: Who *is* that young woman? Her name, we soon learned, was Audrey Kathleen Hepburn-Ruston, she was the daughter of a baroness, and within weeks of the film's release her gamine style, her singular offscreen fashion sense, and even her haircut were copied by a generation of women throughout the world.

At a time when the prevailing notion of the acceptable way for women to dress was highly sexual, with a very obvious silhouette of large breasts, a tiny waist beneath a full skirt, and mincing heels, by her example, Audrey offered another way for women to dress, behave, aspire to, and even be.

And almost fifty-five years since we first saw *Roman Holiday*, Audrey is still showing us how it's done. As a style icon, her influence is unrivaled. In 2006, *New Woman* magazine voted her the Most Beautiful Woman of All Time. On Seventh Avenue, in Hollywood, in the halls of *Vogue*, *People* magazine, or *InStyle*, to describe something (or someone) as "very Audrey" is shorthand for the absolute height of chic.

Today, fashion designers are the new rock stars. On television, shows like *America's Next Top Model* and *Project Runway* attempt to demystify the fashion world, and not an awards show goes by without stars being asked: "What are you wearing?"

But Audrey was—and still is—the first. Every fall or spring, it seems, another designer mimics the clean lines of her crisp white shirt, the little black dress, or beautifully fitted Givenchy-esque suit. Often without realizing it, the best dressed among us are still reveling in the lessons Audrey taught.

When you see someone wearing oversized sunglasses with an evening gown, that's not original—that's Audrey. Ballet flats outside of a dance studio? Audrey was the first. The straight line of a black sweater and fitted black trousers that every fashion editor in the world seems to favor? Way before Prada had fashionistas dressing like they were en route to a beatnik funeral, Audrey was appearing that way—quite radically for the time—in the mid 1950s.

But the way she dressed was almost the least of what makes Audrey cool. Decorator Jeffrey Bilhuber, who has worked with some of the most stylish women of our time, believes that Audrey is still so compelling today because of who she was: "Audrey never systematically schemed to become a star—she had stardom within her . . . it didn't have to be created or manufactured. It was always there. She would have been as admirable a math teacher as she would have been a movie star, because she was predestined for greatness—she was what she was."

Her cultural influence is still so iconic that in September 2006, Gap unveiled the Audrey Hepburn™ Pant to Middle America (much to the chagrin of many of her fans—"nothing less than a travesty," said one fashion blogger—and her more proper Hollywood friends) with a television ad that featured a computer-generated Hepburn dancing to the very non-Audrey AC/DC's "Back in Black." The fact that the campaign was okayed by her sons Sean Ferrer and Luca Dotti, that Gap made a generous donation to the Audrey Hepburn Children's Fund, mollified few people. "They also made her look much thinner than she was in real life," complained a close friend of Audrey's.

As to whether Audrey would or would not have sold herself out like that, the jury is still undecided—had her first marriage to Mel Ferrer not imploded, he might have tried to broker some kind of a deal. But those who knew Audrey knew (as Cary Grant did) that "in spite of her fragile appearance, she's like steel," and doubt she ever would have allowed anything so crassly commercial to occur under her name or image. On the other hand, they know she would have done practically anything to help promote the good work of UNICEF.

Audrey was the first celebrity of her stature to use her fame to help others and, beyond that, to help those whom most people did not care about, or barely thought of. Especially today, when the prevailing notion of celebrity is pure ego satisfaction—"I am famous, therefore I am [and therefore: you owe me]"—and the bar for being considered famous is sinking lower and lower (appearing on a reality television show, being picked up for DUI, having a blog), Audrey could be considered quite radical because she used her fame for something other than her own personal gain.

As Robert Wolders, her companion and spouse in everything but name and her partner during the happiest years of her life, observed, "Audrey sensed at a very early age that fame or stardom doesn't mean that much. So she made a conscious decision within herself—she was very realistic, and aware that she had to do something with this notoriety, this attention she was getting. Something to help others, if she could. And this was something that she was born with."

Today, Audrey's sentiment is increasingly prevalent among the more enlightened celebrities. As Matt Damon recently observed of fame, "I think it's incumbent on us to do as much good as you can within the sphere of influence that you have. Otherwise, it's just a waste of resources."

But before George Clooney and Angelina Jolie, even before Oprah Winfrey was doing so, Audrey and Rob were flying in little planes to some of the most desolate places on earth—Ethiopia, El Salvador and Nicaragua, Sudan, Bangladesh, and finally, Somalia, the one that broke her heart.

Another more interesting question might be: Why, more than fifty years after *Roman Holiday* was released, is Audrey Hepburn still being held up as a style (and in our opinion life) icon? Since we first met Audrey in 1953, and after her untimely death in 1993, she has rarely been off the cultural radar. Robert Wolders thinks the answer is simple (although mildly depressing in the society we find ourselves in today): No one has taken her place.

Oh sure, there have been a few pretenders to the throne (Jacqueline Kennedy Onassis, Grace Kelly, Sofia Coppola), but really, has anyone, could anyone, replace Audrey? We're going to go out on a limb here and say no. But rather than get depressed over this (and the fact that we shall never, in this lifetime and quite possibly the next, be able to eat all the carbs we want and never gain weight), let's study Audrey's life lessons and learn what we can from her.

• • •

As a woman of her influence and stature, Audrey has had dozens of books written about her. Although her face and the on-screen characters she created are famous, there is still much we don't know about Audrey.

Yes, she had a twenty-inch waist that an early Hollywood PR man insisted on encircling in a dog collar as a publicity stunt and having a photographer take a picture of. Hubert de Givenchy remained her friend for life, and was the executor of her estate. Although renowned for her mesmerizing eyes, she did not wear makeup at home. She knew how to iron. She was handy and could fix things. She did not like to drive. Her two divorces almost killed her. She had trouble gaining weight and enjoyed eating bowls of pasta.

And in case you're wondering—she was not an American, and not even distantly related to Katharine Hepburn.

She smoked two—and occasionally three—packs of cigarettes a day her entire adult life, yet had such personal self-discipline that she could eat a square of dark baking chocolate and stop at that. Winner of two Oscars (one posthumously), she was nominated four times and was one of the few people to win an Oscar, a Tony, an Emmy, and a Grammy. But Audrey's real dream was to be a wife and mother. "Even when I was a little girl," she said, "what I wanted most was to have a child. That was always the real me. The movies were fairy tales."

In spite of her memorable, beautiful visage, Audrey did not consider herself attractive. Rob Wolders thought "she was like a child that refused to believe how good she looked." But her friend Audrey Wilder said she must have had some sense of her influence on modern twentieth- and now twenty-first-century fashion. "When she saw so many copies of herself walking down the street, how could she not?" she observed rightly.

But let's not kid ourselves, there are ways that AH was like us, and ways that she was *way* better that we are. Yes, she was born with great beauty, an enviable bone structure, and a manner that made practically everyone she met fall instantly in love with her. She also rarely exercised, ate whatever she wanted, enjoyed a Scotch in the evening, and remained an enviable 110 pounds her entire adult life.

(How did she do it? Don't worry, we'll get to that.)

On the other hand—and this is where the real lessons begin for us—her personal life was not the cakewalk she wanted the world to believe it was. In reality, her experience was full of tremendous heartbreak. ("Until Rob, she just didn't have much luck in the man department, did she?" said Dominick Dunne, a friend.) There were miscarriages, personal betrayals, loneliness, and unfaithful husbands. Still she kept going.

And truth be told, she was not St. Audrey (a term she detested), nor the simple, ethereal princess that Gregory Peck fell in love with.

• • •

Life, wrote the seventeenth-century English philosopher Thomas Hobbes, is "nasty, brutish, and short." Wow. And this was before the invention of CNN, BlackBerry addiction, and Internet dating. Today, politicians (granted, not the most stylish group at any level) are at one another's throats. The stock market is up, or it is down. Etiquette (basic or otherwise) is at an all-time low. Even the people we traditionally look to for fun-loving advice—the Hollywood starlet or her East Coast counterpart, the socialite—are too busy getting arrested, checking into rehab, popping prescription drugs, or neglecting to wear lingerie in public to be of much help to us.

Who, then, can we turn to?

In the beginning of the twenty-first century (much as we did for most of the twentieth century), we look to Miss Audrey for advice. For consolation. For encouragement. For answering the inevitable question: What the heck am I going to wear today?

What follows, then, in one handy volume, is the full Audrey Primer. From beginner lessons (Iron your shirt! Stand up straight!) through the advanced (getting out of that marriage without losing your mind), *What Would Audrey Do?* will show you how to navigate both the shoals and the high points of your life.

WWAD? is not another Hepburn biography, but a primer in what we can learn—today—from Audrey's life lessons. There is Audrey's beauty and style, obviously, but also how to run your life, how to rebound after a brutal divorce. Two brutal divorces. We also explore her interior life, her sensitivity—this is what made her a great actress, after all, but also made her intensely vulnerable to the slights of the world, and Hollywood is a notoriously tough town. How did she keep going?

"Audrey was such a regular, down to earth person, that when I read some of what people write about her, I don't recognize her," says Rob Wolders. With close to ten years of research, interviews with Audrey's friends, family, and those she loved, as well as access to new sources of information, WWAD? is the ultimate Audrey go-to guide.

For those of you who don't know your history—and really, which of us do?—we've got enough biographical information here to satisfy the most devoted Audrey fan. Audrey's place in pop culture? Her role as a cultural icon? How she influences designers and style icons today? All covered. Dating tips from Audrey? Got it. How to get some Audrey Style for yourself? We've got it right here. In short, how to make your way through the vagaries of your own life by using AH's experiences as an example. So instead of merely considering Audrey as a style icon (a simple enough thing), we are going to study the underpinnings of her life as philosophical guideposts for decisions we make in our own lives.

Because face it, while we might not have Audrey's enviable figure (heck, we know we don't), there are still so many lessons we can learn from her. How to overcome adversity. How to create the life that *you* want. How to be a fashion icon in your own corner of the world. (And forget what Hollywood tells you—size has almost nothing to do with it.)

Think of this book as Advanced Audrey, because like Audrey herself, WWAD? is a Zen koan with a soupçon of style thrown in. And because frankly, while she played both a princess and a Givenchy-clad call girl with equal aplomb on-screen, the real Audrey was smarter, tougher (at times), funnier, stronger willed, more vulnerable, earthier, and far more worldly than the public either knew or imagined.

And someday—whether you are a precocious eighth grader, a sorority gal, out in the world and working, dating three guys at once, a stay-at-home mom, or an Oscar-winning actress with a few style issues of your own—you will thank us for lifting the curtain on All Things Audrey. Because really, don't you think we could all use some Audrey in our lives, right now?

TEST YOUR AH IQ . . .

1. Audrey and Katharine Hepburn: related or not?

2. Audrey's early style influence came from _____?

3. When Hubert de Givenchy first met AH, he:
   a. looked forward to creating the greatest design collaboration of the twentieth century.
   b. thought she was someone else.
   c. was too busy designing pocketbooks for Marc Jacobs/LVMH to see her.

4. Audrey's favorite food was:
   a. pasta.
   b. green smoothies.
   c. cold cereal (used years later as an homage by Jerry Seinfeld on his hit TV show).

5. Which of the following did Audrey *not* say:
   a. "How do I look?"
   b. "My mother taught me to stand straight, sit erect, use discipline with wine and sweets, and to smoke only six cigarettes a day."
   c. "I'm taking this home!" (after a photo shoot)

6. Audrey:
   a. was the mother of two boys.
   b. adopted a child from Ethiopia.
   c. had no interest in children.

7. Audrey:
   a. broke her back falling off a horse.
   b. ran three miles a day.
   c. performed all her own stunts.

8. Tales of Audrey's offscreen transgressions abound—true or false?

9. Which star said, "Sure, I loved Audrey, it was easy to love her."
   a. Gregory Peck
   b. George Clooney
   c. Ronald Reagan

10. The following statements are TRUE or FALSE:

Audrey and Jacqueline Kennedy Onassis met each other. (T/F)

When JKO was an editor at Doubleday, she repeatedly called AH and tried to persuade her to write her memoirs. In spite of the entreaties of both Jackie and Audrey's sons, she declined. (T/F)

JFK dated Audrey before he married Jacqueline Bouvier. (T/F)

Please allow one point for each correct answer.

CORRECT ANSWERS:

1. no; 2. lack of funds and the ballet; 3. a; 4. a; 5. c; 6. a; 7. a; 8. FALSE; 9. a; 10. TRUE, TRUE, TRUE.

10 correct—Admit it: You're Jeffrey Banks.

9 correct—Why aren't you writing this book?

7–8 correct—*Genius!*

5 correct—Look at it this way: You are in the upper fiftieth style percentile . . . or something like that.

3 correct—The main thing is that you always try your hardest, and we know AH would agree with us on this point.

1–2 correct—Don't worry, Audrey had to start somewhere, too.

Please note—Cameron Silver, subscribers to *InStyle* magazine, Michael Kors's design staff, and the entire freshman class at FIT are ineligible because they'd better know this stuff already.

chapter 1

Audrey as Movie Star

"I worked my *ass* off."–AH

Audrey Hepburn was a movie star.

It is almost as if the gods had smiled down and chosen *her*. By the age of twenty-five she had survived the Nazis, almost starved to death, kissed Gregory Peck, met Givenchy, been scared as hell, won an Oscar, won a Tony, been engaged, been alone, grown up without her father, been discovered by William Wyler, charmed Colette, posed for a soap ad in London, and been on the cover of *Time* magazine (when appearing on the cover of *Time* meant something).

In short: She was not like us. Because no matter how much they wander around with their T-shirts and Starbucks coffee cups, their sunglasses and baseball caps, movie stars are not like us, they are not meant to be—they are "us" writ large: the us we wish we could be. Like all great women (and men), history smiles down upon them. As the Greeks, successful presidential candidates, and Madison Avenue know: If we did not have heroes, we would create them.

"She struck me as being very alert, very smart, very talented, very ambitious."–William Wyler, upon meeting AH in 1951

BEFORE SHE WAS A STAR

Before they get discovered, some stars land a soap opera gig, like Demi Moore and Alec Baldwin, others walk down Hollywood Boulevard in a chicken suit handing out flyers for a local Mexican restaurant, as did Brad Pitt. Although she was—honestly—practically an overnight success, here is Audrey's verbatim account to powerful Hollywood columnist Hedda Hopper[1] of (some of) what she did in London's West End before her big break.

"In London I did *High Button Shoes* twice nightly for three years. That was twelve times a week, plus ballet classes. Then I did another show twelve times weekly. While in this show, the same producer,

---

[1] New research from a recently discovered nine-page (single-spaced) transcribed interview between AH and HH. Never before seen, this very revealing conversation took place between Hepburn and Hopper on September 11, 1953, at Hopper's office in Hollywood, California.

Cecil Landeau, wanted to do cabaret. He said anybody who'd like to make an extra shilling could be in it. After the show at 11:30 at night, I would go to Ciro's by 12:00, make up, and do another show. All dancing. I would get home by 2:00. I made eleven pounds in the first show; and twenty pounds in the second. So I was doing eighteen shows weekly and earning in American dollars $150 a week. I was completely nuts. The same producer was a very ambitious man—he decided to do a Christmas show in pantomime for children. He called it *Christmas Party*. He asked if we would like to do it. There were four girls and we said, 'Let's.' I must say I was the only one to stay after a week of rehearsals. I would get home by 2:00, eat, and go to sleep. At 10:00 a.m. I would be in rehearsal. I was very ambitious and took every opportunity. I wanted to learn and I wanted to be seen."

In spite of her ethereal aura, Audrey's work ethic was formidable. At this early stage of her career, she was doing twenty-one shows a week in London's West End, and even took on a Christmas show to get (as she put it) "a big fat pay packet." Then, she appeared in the chorus of a light musical, *Sauce Piquant* (and was paid fifteen pounds a week). "An extraordinary thing for me," she recalled. "I was a girl in the chorus but the critics singled me out . . . [I] was astounded to see my name mentioned."

Some of her cast mates were less than thrilled. "I can't stand it," complained a more voluptuous dancer, Aud Johanssen. "I've got the best tits on stage, and yet they're all staring at a girl who hasn't got any."

In September 1951, Audrey's luck was about to change even more when she did a screen test at Pinewood Studios in London for a movie called *Roman Holiday*. The director, William Wyler, said that he was looking for a girl without an American accent, someone you could believe might actually be a princess. They had been looking on two continents, auditioning thousands of would-be Princess Anns, but without success.

Wyler didn't feel like sticking around and conducting the tests himself, so he chose a few girls to be tested for the lead female role and put Thorold Dickinson in charge.

Dickinson had worked with Audrey before in a small British film called *The Secret People*, so he knew what she was capable of. For the test, they did a few scenes from *Roman Holiday*, but since Paramount wanted to see what she was like as a person, he loaded a camera with a thousand feet of film and just let it roll—getting Audrey to speak about the war, the Allied raid on Arnhem, and hiding out in a cellar. It was "a deeply moving thing," he recalled.

At Wyler's request, the camera kept rolling, and someone told Audrey she could leave. She stayed put. "I didn't hear anybody say 'Cut!'" she said. "Only one man here has the right to say 'Cut' and I won't move until I hear him."

"Cut!" said Dickinson. But the camera kept rolling as Audrey sat up in her royal bed, stretched sexily, clasped her hands behind her knees, smiled, and asked how she'd done.

When the results were flown to Wyler in Rome, he found them irresistible. "She had everything I was looking for—charm, innocence, and talent. She was also very funny. She was absolutely enchanting, and we said, 'That's the girl.'"

The studio fired off a cable to Richard Mealand, their representative in London: "Exercise the option on this lady. The test is certainly one of the best ever made in Hollywood, New York or London."

AUDREY: THE BACKSTORY

Audrey Hepburn was born Edda Kathleen van Heemstra Hepburn-Ruston in Brussels on May 4, 1929. Her mother was a Dutch baroness whose own aspirations of becoming an actress and opera singer were discounted by her family because of their place in society. "When I was younger," she once said, "I wanted to be thin, beautiful, and an actress, now isn't it ironic that I have a daughter who's all three?"

Audrey's father, Joseph Hepburn-Ruston, was a charming Anglo-Irish businessman with strong Nazi inclinations. The Hepburn-Rustons had a difficult marriage, made worse by Joseph's support of Hitler, his alcohol abuse, and his eventual decision to channel some of his in-laws' wealth toward fascist causes.

It is said that Audrey, always a sensitive child, hid under the dining room table when her parents argued.

In May 1935, Ruston did the unthinkable: He walked out on his wife and six-year-old daughter on the eve of World War II, leaving them to fend for themselves. The loss of Audrey's father haunted Audrey well into adulthood and her two failed marriages. She considered her father's disappearance "the most traumatic event in my life" and remembered that her mother's hair turned white overnight.

As an adult, Audrey rarely spoke to the press of her childhood or her father. "There was a great deal of pain involved, because, before the war he left us," she recalled. "My mother explained very sweetly that he'd gone on a trip and she didn't think he was coming back. I was terribly jealous of other little girls who did have adoring daddies, and all that."

Talk show host Phil Donohue, in a 1990 interview, asked Audrey if living under the Nazis made her insecure. "That is not what made me insecure," she said. "My father leaving us is what left me insecure. It stayed with me through my own relationships. When I fell in love and got married, I lived in constant fear of being left. . . ."

Despite her father's disappearance, there was joy in young Audrey's life. Growing up in the Dutch town of Arnhem during World War II, she had always loved ballet, which she began studying at the age of eleven. Dance was an escape for Audrey, an attempt to find beauty in an unkind world. As chaotic as the war years were, she always continued with her lessons. It gave a center to her world. In fact, she gathered up the neighborhood children and gave them lessons at her grandfather's home, installing a barre in his large entrance hall with its black and white marble floor. "I gave classes for all ages," she remembered. "I accepted what was about a dime a lesson. We worked to a gramophone wound by hand."

By 1944, as the Germans marched across Europe, Audrey was dancing endless hours in shoes that were worn to shreds but impossible to replace. Finally, she resorted to the only, painful, alternative— wooden ones.

But even the rigorous beauty of ballet could not keep reality at bay. Her mother's family, the van Heemstras, were rumored to be part Jewish, and a favorite uncle and cousin were executed as enemies of the Third Reich. Occupying forces confiscated Audrey's ancestral home and bank accounts. Though just a child, she distributed anti-Nazi literature during the war and barely escaped capture by the Germans.

Even while playing the princess in Hollywood, Audrey never forgot the suffering she and others endured under the Nazis. At fifteen, she was in Holland during "the hunger winter"—the last winter of the war, 1944–45, where so many died of starvation and a tuberculosis epidemic that there was a shortage of caskets. She ate tulip bulbs and tried to make bread from grass. Many days she only had water to drink, and drank a great deal of it in order to feel full, or went to bed in the afternoon in order to conserve her strength.

By the time Holland was liberated, Audrey was five feet six, weighed ninety pounds, and was afflicted with anemia, asthma, jaundice, and other diseases stemming from poor diet. Having suffered from varying degrees of malnutrition from the age of eleven through sixteen, Audrey's metabolism would always be affected by her traumatic adolescence. As an adult, she struggled, always, to keep weight on. While her famous gamine figure would become celebrated in the coming years, it was, in fact, a combination of genes (she had the exact same figure as her father's mother) and tragic circumstance.

Audrey's *Actors Studio* Moment

Audrey never took a single acting lesson in her life. But for all of you actors/models/spokespeople who wonder "How the heck did she do that?"—meaning: Be such an incredible actress?—here is AH on technique. . . .

After Hedda Hopper asked her, "How do you conceive of a part you play?" Audrey responded, "Something happens in you. When you read a book, you make your own interpretation of the characters . . . when I first read a book I see them. It happens very clearly."

Audrey had never had formal training. She studied dance before she did films, and had voice lessons before her *Gigi* appearance on Broadway, to help her voice project beyond the first few rows. But beyond that, it was pure instinct. Or very good natural ability.

"God kissed her on the cheek, and there she was," said Billy Wilder.

MEETING AUDREY:
THE EARLY YEARS

In the Exceptionally Lucky Break Department, Audrey and famed Hollywood photographer Bob Willoughby met one morning in March 1953, after he got a call from his agent asking him to go over to Paramount to cover the publicity shoot of a young ingénue who had just created a big impression with her role in William Wyler's soon-to-be-released film *Roman Holiday*.

Ah—these starlets! They were generally very nice and sincere, and waiting for their big break, like everyone else in L.A., but Bob was hoping for more important assignments. After all, he was twenty-five years old and already shooting for *Harper's Bazaar* and *Look*.

Bob was ambitious. He wanted to see the world, move on to bigger things, maybe head to Paris, do some artsy stuff. But, his agent reminded him, it was these assignments, usually for fan magazines—the precursors of *Us Weekly* and *People* and *InStyle*—that kept him in food, film, and darkroom equipment.

"Bob—you're poor and you need money and get your ass over there," his agent said bluntly, as any good ten-percenter should.

So Willoughby packed up his cameras and headed over to the Stills Gallery on the lot. There, he caught up with Bud Fraker, the head portrait photographer.

While waiting for their subject, a vision floated out of the dressing room. Fraker caught Bob's eye—"She's something, isn't she?"

Bob was so taken aback at her beauty that his jaw practically hit the floor.

Yes.

So that explained why Paramount was going all out with the phalanx of publicists and makeup and wardrobe people; even the studio's head designer, Edith Head, was there. Obviously, this entire setup was a big deal. This young woman—whoever she was—was not just another hungry nobody from the Midwest with a ninth-grade education and perfect skin. Bud set up behind the huge eight-by-ten studio portrait camera as Bob sorted out his own shots.

It was only during a break in shooting that someone thought to introduce them: "Bob, this is Audrey Hepburn."

Miss Hepburn, just a year younger than Bob, took his hand and smiled with an energy fated to melt men's hearts. Like almost everyone else who met Audrey, Bob practically fell in love with her on the spot. His early apathy turned to enthusiasm. It was only later, after seeing *Roman Holiday*, that he realized she really was the princess she portrayed.

Bob went home that night and tried to describe Audrey to his mother, but it was hard to convey her magic.

He had met the most unique young woman today. . . . "She's in a movie, *Roman Holiday*, with Greg Peck. She plays a princess, and word on the lot is that Peck insisted she get top billing alongside him—otherwise, he told his agent, he's going to look like an idiot. And she's a complete unknown!"

Wait, he told his mother, wait. "Let me develop the prints and you'll see what I mean." It was hard to put it into words, but he had a feeling that knowing this girl would change his life.

Whatever *it* was, she had it.

Audrey and Stardom: What *Was* It?

When Audrey first graced the screen as the princess in *Roman Holiday*, her early life was far more harrowing than she let on, and she was also a good deal more ambitious—and strong willed—than she appeared. Below, some star setting tips for everyone.

Rule No. 1:
Be Memorable

As a star, or even as an unforgettable person making your way in the world, you do *not* want to be like everyone else.

Even at a young age, Audrey knew what worked for her and what didn't. She had a very strong vision of her place in the world and, in this sense, was very much like a princess. Robert Wolders observed, "She was secure in her values and early on found a level where she felt and functioned best. Her personal style was a result of her unwillingness to compromise on those values and to focus on what is basic and real. She showed a good deal of stubbornness toward outside influences, always insisting on what felt natural and comfortable.

"Her sense of appropriateness and decorum was happily mixed with a sense of irony and humor—not taking yourself too seriously, but seriously enough."

Rule No. 2:
Be Modest

It sounds like an oxymoron, doesn't it? Stand out in the crowd and be modest. But in addition to her will and ambition (and a talent that she was perhaps only beginning to recognize), Audrey had a very real modesty that was encouraged by her upbringing. A modesty that was rare to come by—and not at all encouraged in Hollywood. Her professional ascent was swift and decisive, and she had a great deal to brag about. In the following year she would win a Tony Award for *Ondine*, a play she was performing on Broadway, and both an Oscar and a Golden Globe Award for *Roman Holiday*.

Still, Audrey never forgot where she came from. This core of certainty was one of her strengths. Years later, she would remember something her mother said to her—" 'Considering that you have no talent, it's really extraordinary where you've got.' She said it in the middle of all the lovely successes I was having. She wasn't putting me down," Audrey reasoned. "She was saying how fortunate I was."

Rule No. 3:
Maintain a Sense of Wonder About
Your Life and the World

Having survived World War II and then landed in Hollywood, Audrey was lucky as hell, and she knew it. One might ask, did she have any sense of what the impact of *Roman Holiday* might be when she made it?

"Not at all," said Audrey, "I had no sense, period! I was awfully new and awfully young to be doing my first movie, and thrilled to be doing it. But I was not even aware of the significance of doing a picture with William Wyler—who William Wyler really was. . . . He came to England, looking for an unknown for the picture, which in fact was my only qualification."

On some level, though, she knew that her life was about to change. Audrey's response when she learned of Paramount's decision to cast her as the lead in *Roman Holiday* was touching in its simplicity: "Lord, help me live up to all of this."

• • •

Modest. Extremely talented. Strong willed. Shy. Beautiful. Disciplined. Hidden. Audrey was all of these things and more. "The test of a first rate intelligence," wrote F. Scott Fitzgerald, "is the ability to hold two opposed ideas in the mind at the same time, and still retain the ability to function." Maybe these conflicting dichotomies are what made Audrey such a compelling personality.

BE A MOVIE STAR IN YOUR OWN LIFE

While you might not be discovered by William Wyler, or have above-the-title billing with Gregory Peck (on your first major movie), we can all learn from AH—some advice on how to be a star in our own life. And then pass the magic on.

Take yourself seriously. Audrey was lighthearted, but never silly. Modest, but not lacking in confidence. It doesn't matter where you are on the food chain—the point is to imbue yourself with the grace and guts that Audrey had. And move forward.

We know we are asking you to walk a fine line here: Take yourself seriously (but not *too* seriously). Because if you don't, no one will.

You are a star—act like one. Again and again, in speaking with the people who worked with Audrey (on her films, during photo shoots, for UNICEF), they said that you met her once, and you never forgot it.

Tzetzi Ganev, the legendary designer with Western Costume in Los Angeles who worked with Edith Head and practically every star of the mid to late twentieth century—Julie Andrews ("the top of the top"), Lauren Bacall, Greer Garson, Deborah Kerr ("fabulous"), Anjelica Huston, Natalie Wood, Liz Taylor, Barbra Streisand, Bette Davis ("a tough lady. She would chew the director to pieces if she didn't like something")—says that "the ladies of that time were so well groomed. They were so well *prepared*—they were made up, and their hair was done, the high heels they were going to wear, and their makeup, and the stockings!

"Now there is no such thing—actresses today they come without makeup for fittings, without proper underwear, without shoes, the proper heels, they say—oh I forgot! I forgot the bra, so they come without the bra, and they don't have the bra they are going to wear!"

Tzetzi shakes her head. "Stars today just don't know how to behave. . . ."[2]

Surround yourself with great people.

Audrey was well-mannered, but she generally got what she wanted, and that is because she surrounded herself, professionally, with people who operated at a very high level. When Hedda Hopper asked her about the details of her Paramount contract, she said, "I have no regrets. I had very good agents. I think if I deserve more money, I'll get it. I have a very happy contract." Her agent, the former boxer Kurt Frings, was (according to Audrey's first husband, Mel Ferrer) a "devoted and fanatical defender of her interests."

Move beyond your fears.

In spite of the grace and calm that she portrayed on-screen or while giving a speech in public, Audrey suffered from stage fright her entire life. In 1991, she was honored by the Film Society of Lincoln Center, and Ralph Lauren was with her backstage before she walked out to give her acceptance speech. He remembered her as being so nervous, "pacing back and forth."

The director of the tribute, Wendy Keys, has a similar recollection. If there was just one moment she could keep in her mind, it was AH walking onstage. "She threw her shoulders back, and this beautiful white chiffon skirt swirled around her legs as she walked out to greet those people who were so thrilled to see her. It was heightened by the fact that she was so nervous. The sight of her back, with that beautiful French twist and those shoulder blades like nobody else's — it was a moment I'll never get over."

---

[2] For the record, Julia Roberts is one of the few modern stars Tzetzi has high marks for.

Have a vision. Even at a very young age, Audrey had an instinct for what worked for her and what didn't. Develop yours. And not to get too New Agey or anything, but before you walk onto that stage, into that boardroom, onto that airplane, take a few minutes, sit quietly, center yourself, and think about what it is that you want to accomplish. Then, feel it, really feel it—and allow the experience into your life.

Look the part. We will get to the specifics of this later, but Audrey said that when she wore Givenchy's clothing, she felt protected. As a struggling chorus girl starting out in London, she understood the power of clothes (She had just one scarf, which she "knew how to tie seventeen different ways," recalled a friend). And with the first money she earned as an actress—a small role in *Monte Carlo Baby*, shot in May 1951—she bought her first piece of couture, a Givenchy coat.

Hire a good publicist. Birth, Marriage, and Death—in the old days, that's how often members of society wanted to be in the press. Now, with the advent of cable television, youtube, *Us Weekly*, Perez Hilton, video stalkarazzi, the *Forbes* list, IPOs, gawker.com, the opportunities to end up in the media are endless. Is this a good thing? Probably not. All the *stuff* we know about celebrities and our public figures today is just noise. And once the press gets a hold of you, they can lift you up, but they can also—and probably will—be the first to drag you down, as we see in the increasingly public dramas of Britney, Lindsay, Paris, etc. Being a publicity hound can backfire, so choose your appearances carefully.

For this reason (among others), AH generally disliked dealing with the press. She was just too private a person and, as she became more famous, grew wary of the intrusive questions she was forced to endure (mostly about the state of her marriage to Mel—or lack thereof). In fact, once she married her second husband, Dr. Andrea Dotti, in 1969, and moved to Rome, she limited interviews to half an hour because she believed that after that, the reporter would start asking personal questions.

But—and here is her dichotomy—if she had to promote a movie, or a good cause like UNICEF, she was more than happy to speak to the press, because she knew she could use her fame to do some good.

How to Stay Out of the *New York Post*'s Page Six

Up-and-coming stars of today, take note: Richard Johnson is the charming and exceedingly well dressed editor of Page Six, the influential (and occasionally feared) gossip column that is the first thing celebrities, former presidents, Ford models, and media movers and shakers on both coasts—and either side of the Atlantic—read each morning

If you behave yourself, you have nothing to worry about—in fact, a Page Six mention can be considered a positive. But if you end up on his wrong side, or in a holding cell downtown without Bert Fields's number on speed dial—watch out. Fortunately, Audrey never had to worry about embarrassing items showing up on Page Six. As Johnson recalls, "We didn't write much about her when she was alive, because she didn't do much besides her humanitarian work—she was a perfect lady. And Robert Wolders, her companion at the end, was a well-mannered, well-dressed man who knew how to handle things. I was impressed."

And if you don't hire a publicist, be your own good publicist.
If you are about to do something in public, ask yourself, "What would Audrey do?" And if that doesn't give you pause, think about how it would look on the front page of the *New York Post* or the *National Enquirer*. And act accordingly.

Throw a tantrum once in a while. Okay, AH never did this, but if you occasionally throw a tantrum, it can be extremely memorable, especially if you don't normally behave like a diva. The only known instance of Audrey behaving badly[3] was during the extremely arduous filming of *My Fair Lady*. She had been training nonstop for several months, in addition to singing lessons, dancing lessons, elocution lessons with a professor from UCLA, putting up with Rex Harrison's ego, and practically carrying the entire picture herself. One fateful day, the musical director, André Previn—possibly taking pity on all of her hard work—finally let her know that her singing voice was not going to be used in the film.[4] She said, "Oh," walked off the set, out the door, and went home.

The next day she returned and apologized.

Don't be afraid to disappear. From the way she naturally conducted her life, Audrey understood the inherent appeal of not making yourself too available . . . to the press, your fans, that guy who wants a date on Saturday night. She also realized that you need to take time out for yourself. In the middle of an arduous day of shooting, Audrey would skip the commissary and have a quiet lunch in her dressing room—even if it did cause one (male) columnist to accuse her of being stuck-up. She felt that she needed to conserve her energy and not fritter it away socializing.

---

[3] For *Audrey*, we mean.
[4] Instead, her singing would be dubbed by Marni Nixon, although AH can be heard in the restored 1994 MFL print.

When she was single, after a long week on the lot, Audrey would occasionally hole herself up in her apartment on weekends, reading, resting, and listening to her beloved jazz records, and just gearing up for the week to come. So don't be afraid to disappear for a while. In other words, leave them wanting more.

Don't trade on your personal tragedies. Audrey certainly had some heartbreak in her life—life during WWII; her father leaving her mother when she was six years old—but she did not dwell on it. And she very pointedly did not dwell on it in the press to score points, raise her Q Score (frankly, she didn't have to), jump on Oprah's couch, or promote whatever movie she was in at the time.

Audrey kept her private life and her public life separate. Something we would all do well to keep in mind these days.

Be enigmatic. A natural sense of discretion will give you the reputation of being enigmatic. This is very good for a movie star, and you, to emulate. It also makes people wonder and, who knows, just might even raise your stock.

Live the part. When Audrey was starting out, she had very little money. By the time she was a world-famous movie star in the late 1950s, she was buying Famous, her Yorkie, diamond collars at Van Cleef & Arpels. Clearly, she understood the role of the starlet and could look—and live—the part. Buy quality, not quantity.

DEALING WITH THE PRESS

Instinctively—like so much else she did—Audrey was genius with the care and feeding of the press. And, like it or not, dealing with the media is often a part of our modern lives. You might decide to run for president, you might win *American Idol*, you might be involved in a coup d'état with the PTA. In any event, there is a very good chance that you, like Audrey, could find yourself at the receiving end of an interview. Herewith, a few things to tilt the odds in your favor.

Charm the beast. Audrey was so successful with the press because she was always, most notably, herself. Whether being interviewed by Hedda Hopper early in her career, or a *People* magazine reporter in the late 1980s, she was always light, funny, focused, and charming.

When dealing with the press, charm is your ally. Be lighthearted, be charismatic. Pretend it's a first date. Build rapport with the reporter—seduce the heck out of him/her (metaphorically speaking, of course)—you're a movie star, after all! When in doubt, use the George Clooney rather than the Russell Crowe model. While truculence looks great on the screen or while shooting a Calvin Klein print ad, it was a tone that AH never adopted, and gets tiresome in a one-on-one interview. Remember: You're the one who wanted to be a star, so don't bail out now.

Whether you choose the patented Tom Cruise "Hey, isn't life wonderful?" high energy/laugh a lot through the entire interview and reveal nothing technique, or the enigmatic "I am an artist" Pacino mode, make sure you have a game plan going in.

Also, it helps to know that unless you are being interviewed by the *Wall Street Journal*, Anderson Cooper, or Diane Sawyer, most reporters are really lazy and don't do their homework. (They never did any in school, why start now?) And entertainment "reporters" are probably the worst. Use their inherent slackerdom (*very* non-Audrey, we might add) to your advantage. With some effort, you can almost chart what the questions might be, so have a few responses ready.

And if you really get stuck for an answer, smile winningly and then say, "Boy, that's a great question. . . ." And leave it at that.

Ditch the PR person. You didn't get where you are by following the rules. With the reporter standing by, tell your corporate PR flunky that you "can handle this" and show them the door. This will make you look like a maverick and will create a false sense of intimacy between you and the reporter. A false sense of intimacy that you will, of course, exploit fully to your advantage.

Keep them at arm's distance. If you are a world-famous actress, physical separation is terrific for keeping the press hounds at bay. During her off hours, living in a small village in Switzerland, rather than Bel-Air, and being generally inaccessible was Audrey's way of dealing with the picayune attention that came with having one of the most recognizable faces in the world.

Just say no. The first time AH was supposed to be interviewed by Barbara Walters in 1971, she turned her down because she had not heard of her and did not want to answer personal questions. In the years that followed, Barbara became a bit more well known, and AH was interviewed by her in 1989.

Hold your ground. No matter what the reporter asks, always hold your ground and answer the question that you want to answer. In a rare filmed interview following a 1963 press conference announcing the making of *My Fair Lady* on the Warner lot, the reporter repeatedly tries to corner Audrey and put words in her mouth. She waits, thinks, sometimes asks him to clarify his question, occasionally gives him a dazzling smile, and answers exactly what she wants. It is quite a performance.

When dealing with the press, the main thing is: Don't be intimidated; hold your ground, and try to have as clear a sense as possible of what you want to say before you go on—that way, you will make sure that you get your point across.

Ask for final edit. If you are on a news program, ask if you can have final edit. Unless you are Bill Clinton, it is very unlikely you will ever get this, but what the heck—it can't hurt to ask. Conversely, find out if the show is live, or live to tape. Although (possibly) more nerve-racking, this is potentially better for you, since the producers cannot edit your comments to make you look silly. Given the kinder media era she grew up in, Audrey never had to worry about any of this.

Don't live in the press. There are some people (you know who you are) who live to be in the media. They could be Madonna, they could be the owner of the local car dealership who never met a reporter he did not like. Remember, if you live by the sword, you will die by the sword, so the best thing to do is either stay out of the press as much as possible or use it to your advantage only when you want to, as AH did.

On the Red Carpet (or Elsewhere)

Kevin Mazur is one of the preeminent photographers today—a celeb favorite (and all-around nice guy), he has shot Bruce Springsteen, Sting, U2, Dylan, JLo, and Marc Anthony, among others. A regular contributor to the pages of *Rolling Stone* and *Us Weekly*, he is often the only outsider allowed backstage and on the red carpet at major celebrity events.

Although Audrey never needed any advice about looking great for the camera, here are Kevin's tips for the rest of us.

1. "Have fun! If you have fun with the camera and enjoy yourself, it shows!"

2. "Position yourself sideways to the camera. Don't stand straight on, that makes you look flat and heavy. Twist your hips and shoulders."

3. "Try a bunch of different poses—someone like Audrey was always great on the red carpet because she really knew how to pose. She gave photographers a lot to work with—she could look serious, smile, look sexy, all within about five minutes."

4. "Before a big event (say, a wedding), study magazines like *Us* or *People* and see how your favorite stars pose, and what might work for you. Then try them yourself."

5. "You want to raise your chin a little, in case you have a few extra pounds; you don't want any 'wattle' under the neck. But don't tilt your head too high, it will look odd." Practice in front of a mirror if you must

6. Finally, stars are comfortable in front of the camera because it's part of their job. . . . Emulate them—and remember, the camera is your *friend*. Be like Audrey: Use your eyes and flirt with it a little.

7. Again, Kevin reiterated that the main thing is "to have fun with it. Enjoy yourself—that's the main thing. If you do, that will come across in the pictures."

WOULD AUDREY . . .

Sign autographs? Yes. Within reason. When she shot *Gardens of the World with Audrey Hepburn* for PBS in 1990, executive producer Janis Blackschlager remembers her stopping briefly to sign autographs in front of the Plaza Athénée when she stayed there. "There were always people waiting out front, with thirty-year-old pictures," she recalled. "And Audrey got a kick out of seeing them again."

Be extremely low-key? You bet. A friend (granted, a rather clueless friend) was recently seated next to an older gentleman with beautiful blue eyes at a dinner party. "And what do you do?" she asked politely. "Oh, I sell salad dressing," he replied.

A few moments later she realized: Paul Newman.

Although it was practically impossible for her to go unrecognized as Mr. Newman sometimes could, Audrey was the same way.

Care what people said about her on the Internet? No. AH would never have Googled herself. For starters, she would probably be a little freaked out at her extreme popularity (2,110,000 pages in English alone, and counting—and that's not even including Japan or China).

Would the blogs have affected her? Would she have read something like TMZ, gawker, or (god forbid) Perez Hilton on the Internet? No.

Throw her weight around? (such as it was) No. She didn't have to. Because of her inherent grace (or star quality, or upbringing), people tended to listen to Audrey when she spoke. If anything, she was the anti-diva.

There is only one known instance of Audrey even mildly pulling rank, ever, and that was on the set of *Two for the Road*. Audrey and Albert Finney and Stanley Donen, the director, were ready to roll, and production was being held up for some reason. What was the delay? Audrey wondered. Jacqueline Bisset (in one of her first acting jobs) was having problems with her makeup and was not quite ready.

"Yes, but *I'm* ready," Audrey said quietly.

And . . . action.

Answer her own telephone? Absolutely. Social chronicler Dominick Dunne was with her in her hotel suite in the 1980s in New York City and he remembers her picking up her own calls, "Hel-*lo*" in her melodic voice. Her friends still miss that voice.

HEPBURN VS. HEPBURN

Although the two Hepburns—Katharine and Audrey—were confused throughout their lives (and still are today), these screen icons could not have been more dissimilar.[5] Kate barreled through life doing exactly as she pleased for ninety-six years. She had zero interest in marriage, Republicans, or wearing sunblock, didn't care whom she ticked off, and smoked three packs a day for twenty years before giving it up by going cold turkey at the age of forty.

While she trumpeted her originality, Katharine Hepburn is a distinct American archetype. Invariably described as being of New England stock, a *Mayflower* descendant, and more than a little intimidating (think Queen Elizabeth II, Joan Crawford in *Mildred Pierce*, or Barbara Bush), these are not women who need our help. They're blue-blood tough guys: reserved, unironic, and often married to much handsomer men they terrorize into submission with their intelligence, cojones, fierce backhand, and Mummy's charitable lead trust on their side.

While Hepburn was known for her style—Those trousers! Those turtlenecks! Those cheekbones and graceful stride!—these gals are not. Well, they might possess style of a sort (i.e., the Church Lady,

---

[5] When AH signed her first Paramount contract for *Roman Holiday*, the studio asked her to change her surname. She politely refused.

or Talbots circa 1973), but this is not the first thing that comes to mind when their names come up. Given to A-line skirts, triple-strand pearls, and sensible shoes, they are emotionally reserved, opinionated, arch—and you can bet they'll let you know exactly how they feel on any given topic, be it the presidential race, what color to paint the sunroom, the best way to fire the help, or how to raise your children.

With her modesty, grace, less sartorially tomboyish fashion sense, and—dare we say it?—inherent European sophistication, Audrey is the anti-Kate. Because while people might be in awe of the indomitable Miss Kate, they truly love Audrey.

Herewith, a handy clip-and-save guide to tell them apart:

	AUDREY H.	KATHARINE H.
Full name	Audrey Kathleen Hepburn-Ruston	Katharine Houghton Hepburn
DOB	May 4, 1929	May 12, 1907
Sexual inclination	Heterosexual	Bisexual (learned only after biographer A. Scott Berg spilled the beans after her death)
Famously wore pants?	Yes—trim, cropped, and black	Yes—generally high-waisted, tweed, and full-cut
Played scratch golf and tennis, skied, rode horseback, swam in frigid Long Island Sound during winter months	No, no, no, and no	Yes
Height	5'7"	5'7"
Bad reviews?	Never	In a theater review for *The New Yorker*, Dorothy Parker said she "ran the gamut of emotions from A to B."
Charitable organizations	UNICEF	Planned Parenthood
Romantically involved with genius, reclusive billionaire who flew airplanes, owned TWA, lived in hotels for 180 days at a time to avoid paying taxes, later owned most of Las Vegas, and hired Mormons as his trusted aides before descending into unfortunate (but very cinematic) madness. Biopic later brought to the screen by Martin Scorsese and played by Leonardo DiCaprio.	Um, no	Yes, Howard Hughes
Became pen pals after AH failed to receive Oscar nom for *My Fair Lady* (introduced by George Cukor)	Yes	Yes
In true Bryn Mawr style, took cold shower every morning	No, preferred warm, relaxing bath with L'Interdit or Floris poured in it	Yes, believing that it strengthened her constitution
Featured in Gap ad?	Yes	No, not yet
Oscar nominations/Oscars won	5 nominations, 1 win, + 1 awarded posthumously (accepted by son Sean)	12 nominations, 4 wins (Meryl Streep holds record for 14 noms)
Had giant Sotheby's estate sale after her death?	No	Yes, raised $3 million; most of proceeds went to siblings and ABC newscaster Cynthia McFadden
Traumatic event(s) of childhood?	Father abandoning her and mother; surviving WWII; witnessing Nazi occupation	Suicide/accidental death of brother Tom under mysterious circumstances
Children?	2	No
Fashion icon still influencing American designers (see Ralph Lauren, Michael Kors, Burberry, Oscar de la Renta, etc.)	Yes	Yes
"Prickly" personality?	No	Yes
Loved fresh flowers?	Yes	Yes
Relationship with parents?	Overlooked a lot	Adored them both
Perfume created for?	Yes	No
One of a kind, still memorable today, puts most current actors to shame?	Absolutely	Absolutely

chapter 2

Romance Central

"I have more sex appeal on the tip of my nose than many women have in their entire bodies. It doesn't stand out a mile, but it is there."–AH

Audrey's dating life was, like her, both discreet and a heck of a lot of fun. By twenty-four she had already been engaged to (and ended it with) English businessman James Hanson, was on the fence about marrying *über* male Mel Ferrer, was madly, madly in love with Hollywood's resident bad boy William Holden, and was going on the occasional date with Senator John F. Kennedy from Massachusetts. (Mary Gallagher, a secretary in his office, remembers that "the whole office was impressed when she walked in. She was as graceful as a swan and carried a long, slim, red umbrella.")

Still, like so much else, Audrey conducted her personal life with a great deal of élan. Did she ever question that the man in her life was not madly in love with her and did not want to marry her . . . like, yesterday? Did she sit around on Saturday night, waiting for the phone to ring? Did she ever try on an evening dress and ask her significant other, "Does this make me look fat?" *Please.*

She's Audrey.

For Audrey, love was very important. As she admitted, "I was born with an enormous love of people, of children. I loved them when I was little! I used to embarrass my mother by trying to pick babies out of prams at the market." In a later interview in *Vogue*, she wondered, "What makes two people happy? It's like fingerprints: Each one is different. Personally, I need a lot of loving, being loved and giving love. Real love. After that, the rest takes care of itself."

But on the other hand, given her childhood, she already knew a great deal of loss and death, and the inherent uncertainty of the human experience. After her father left her mother, she knew one hard reality: "Whatever you love most, you fear you might lose."

This was Audrey's dichotomy—the princess who had experienced such heartbreak, such death and fear and loss, and kept going. The smiling, graceful young woman with the old soul. The modest girl who seemed to have no sense of her beauty and her talent, who was on the verge of having the world and all its possibilities laid at her feet.

Although first known for her "style," that shorthand phrase that does little to convey the depth of a person, Audrey was a combination of vulnerability and strength of character. Perhaps this, even more than the ballet flats or cropped black pants she is known for, is the source of our lasting intrigue in her. Like many creative people, Audrey had deep reserves of emotional need that she was not afraid to tap into.

As she herself put it, "It always boils down to the same thing—not only receiving love, but wanting desperately to give it, a need to give it!"

And it is, perhaps, this emotional courage that draws us to her still.

But while we might not win an Oscar our first time out of the gate, or date Bill Holden (or who is his modern equivalent—George Clooney? Jamie Foxx?), there are still many lessons that Audrey can teach us in the romance department.

The Pregame Warm-up

How did Audrey get ready for a date? As a single, twenty-four-year-old young woman about town, she admitted:

"I like to have a good hour [to dress for a party]. I take a slow bath, make up, and dress. Then I go to the party and forget about my appearance. Later in the evening I go to the powder room, look in the mirror, and say, 'My God, this is what I've been looking like all evening.' I like parties if I feel like going. Night clubs occasionally for dancing. It's fun if there's someone you want to spend the time with. I prefer quiet evenings."

Keep it light. We believe dating is the most Audrey-esque experience you can have. For starters, look at your life through the prism of Audrey Hepburn and think of all the wonderful adventures you'll have—zipping through Rome on the back of a Vespa, browsing through Tiffany's with that handsome writer, going from being a dowdy Greenwich Village bookworm to the toast of Paris (well, it could happen). In your Audrey Dating World, keep your options open—you never know what might happen next.

For this reason (like AH), we love dating, and—at least until you have a ring on your finger—advocate dating a bunch of people in your singlehood. In our opinion, dating is the time to be most like

Audrey—have fun! Be compelling! Keep your eyes peeled for your own handsome costar.

Audrey met her first serious beau, James Hanson, in the summer of 1950, after she had finished *The Lavender Hill Mob,* a comedy where she made a minor appearance—one sentence long—with Alec Guinness. She is Chiquita, in an airport lounge, where Guinness calls her over and hands her a wad of bills: "Oh, but how *sweet* of you," she coos, and gives him a thank-you kiss on the forehead.

Hepburn and Hanson immediately hit it off. Audrey was twenty-two. Jimmy was twenty-eight, six feet four, and the multimillionaire scion of a Yorkshire trucking industry company. He had served heroically in WWII (at the age of seventeen), from 1939 to its end, with the Duke of Wellington's regiment in North Africa, Italy, and Greece. Back safely from the war, he dressed impeccably, owned his own plane, and frequented the best nightspots of London and New York. He loved beautiful women, in particular, actresses. Most recently, he had been seen about town with Jean Simmons, but that was quickly forgotten once Audrey entered the picture.

As Hanson recalled, "We met at a cocktail party in Mayfair at Les Ambassadeurs, a very popular place, and we were attracted to each other right away. I invited her for lunch next day, and we soon fell in love, became engaged a few months later. She was a one-man woman, and it was a relationship of that kind. We became extremely good friends. Everybody saw in her this wonderful life and brightness and terrific strength of character. She was a very strong young woman who clearly had the determination she was going to need in order to achieve what she did. She had done a couple of small parts in movies, and her career was just about to blossom. There was no doubt about that by anybody who saw her."

Audrey as dating coach. "Discretion is the better part of valor," said Shakespeare's Falstaff. In this regard, take the numero uno Love Lesson from Audrey and keep your personal affairs (largely) to yourself. We're not saying don't have a girly lunch with Connie Wald[6] out by the pool. We're just saying don't go on *Oprah Winfrey* and jump up and down on the couch the next time you fall in love.

Brooke Astor, herself an Audrey-esque paragon of virtue and coolness, never spoke about that sort of thing. "How many loves have you had?" someone had the temerity to ask her in her later years. And she had the equal temerity not to answer. She would never say, she responded cheerfully, "that's how I count myself to sleep."

Don't reveal your hand. A further corollary of this is: "No daylight on magic" (as Cecil Beaton so famously advised the royal family — a lesson they have since so famously forgotten). As an actress, as a European brought up in a "nice" (albeit fractured) home, as an essentially private person, Audrey knew that there was no reason to let everyone see the workings behind the grace. Hubert de Givenchy, one of her closest friends, described her as "shy . . . if she had worries she would not show them."

In this era of the Barbara Walters confessional and *People* magazine tell-all, discretion is such a rarity that a little mystery goes a long way.

The attractor factor. Everyone we spoke to loved Audrey. Everyone. Robert Wolders, the photographers she worked with, seamstresses from Western Costume in L.A., a guy who had lunch with her at a picnic table during a film shoot and spoke with her for about fifteen minutes. People met Audrey and never forgot her.

As her friend Jeffrey Banks admitted, "You looked into her eyes and found yourself basically agreeing with everything she said."

Now, we can't give you the specific formula for being so charismatic. Part of it might be her history. Part of it, certainly, has to be her beauty. But Audrey took a genuine interest in whomever she was speaking to. As Bob Willoughby recalled, "Audrey was not one of those Hollywood types

---

[6] One of Audrey's best friends.

to have a conversation with you, and spent the entire time looking over your left shoulder to see who else had just come in the room."

We're not naming any names here, but if there is the slightest possibility that you are ever guilty of this, keep Audrey in mind when you go to your next cocktail party.

And consider yourself warned.

Juggling lessons from a world-famous actress. Okay, you've

attracted a bunch of promising dating possibilities, but how do you keep them from bumping into one another on your radar screen? Simple, you just do. We're not saying lie or be deceitful to those you are spending time with (very non-AH), we're just saying that some information is definitely on a need-to-know basis. For example, while shooting *Sabrina*, Audrey dated JFK, kept Mel on the back burner in New York City, fell madly in love with her costar, William Holden, and still found time to star in a movie with Humphrey Bogart.

That's our girl.

Audrey and Mel Ferrer were introduced by Gregory Peck, who knew him when they started up the prestigious La Jolla Playhouse together. Tall, hyperactive, hyperenergetic, and hyper (*hyper hyper hyper*) ambitious, Mel was an actor, a radio, stage, and film director (and performer), poet, raconteur, hustler, legendary know-it-all, Hollywood adviser to Howard Hughes, Princeton graduate, and possibly the first member of the Social Register to appear as a hoofer in the chorus of a Broadway musical, *You'll Never Know.*[7]

There was almost too much talent for one man to contain! Born a dozen years before Audrey, in Elberon, New Jersey, on August 25, 1917, he had spent most of his early life in New York City. His father, Dr. José Ferrer, a prominent Cuban-Spanish surgeon at St. Vincent's Hospital in New York City, died when Mel was four.

---

[7] His mother promptly had him removed from the SR once she learned of his new career.

Audrey and Mel met in July 1953, at a party in London, where Audrey had returned for the premiere of *Roman Holiday*. Married three times, twice to the same woman,[8] the father of four was instantly attracted to Audrey. "It was fascinating to watch Mel move in on Audrey," remembered Radie Harris, a respected Hollywood journalist who had known him since 1936. "After that first meeting [with Audrey], Mel never let go, and they were inseparable."

Audrey soon fell in love with the sensitive, soulful character he portrayed in the movie *Lili*. She also loved his voice, and the way he jokingly signed his name "Mellifluous."

Assess the field. We're not saying act like Field Marshal Rommel here, but when you are in the midst of dating a bevy of beaux, or trying to winnow the field, try to take a clear look at the situation and make the decision that is best for you.

When Audrey became involved with her *Sabrina* costar, William Holden, he was thirty-five years old, warm, handsome, charming as hell—no matter what happened, Holden was one of those guys who would *always* be charming as hell—and at the peak of his career, having just starred in two of Billy Wilder's greatest pictures, *Sunset Boulevard* and *Stalag 17*.

Audrey did not let the fact that he was a renowned ladies' man, unhappily married to his long- (very long-) suffering wife, Ardis, or had the beginning of a brutal alcohol addiction, stop her from falling in love with him. ("We could make beautiful babies together," she said.) But once things got serious and she learned that he had had a vasectomy and could not father any more children, she quietly put an end to it, as she knew they would never marry.

For Audrey, marriage and children was a deal breaker. And she was always clear that that was what she wanted.

---

[8] And currently married when they met.

Go easy on accepting gifts. Okay, this might just be us, and we are fairly old-fashioned, but we think it is slightly déclassé to be overly enthusiastic (or suggestive, or demanding) about accepting big-ticket items from boyfriends and admirers.

Of course, once you are engaged or married, all bets are off. Jewelry, artwork, the occasional horse or drum set, a bouquet of daisies handed to you over a picnic blanket in the park—all are welcomed tokens of affection.

But the Cartier watch Mr. Wonderful gave you for Christmas, when what you really wanted was a four-carat stunner? We don't want to advise you on how to play your hand, but if you really want to make a statement, try handing the little red leather box back to him and say-ing "no thanks." Without saying very much—that's saying something.

Plus, these days it is cooler to buy your own bling, if for no other reason than to show the world that you can.

And while we love Jackie, she was far more avaricious than our Audrey. When a man was dating JKO, particularly if he was a Greek shipping tycoon, he was expected to put up the goods. The first time she spent time on the *Christina* (when she was First Lady and Ari was ostensibly dating her sister, Lee), Ari saw the meager (to his mind) state of Jackie's jewelry selection and immediately summoned Van Cleef & Arpels in Paris and presented her with a stunning ruby and diamond bracelet.

Lee was heartbroken and JFK furious, but Jackie nonchalantly wore it back to the White House when she returned.

Clearly, very non-AH behavior.

As a widow in NYC, Jackie accepted substantial donations from Bunny Mellon, Robert F. Kennedy, Lazard Frères moneyman André Meyer, and Ari, all to help purchase her apartment at 1040 Fifth Avenue. An amount that could have bought the apartment several times over.

Again (and we are not making any judgments here), very non-AH behavior. Perhaps it was her experiences during WWII (or her

European upbringing), but Audrey was not very materialistic. Yes, she liked nice things, but she was not flashy, or showy.

Closing the deal.

Ladies (and men), don't be afraid to put your cards on the table and ask for what you want. A good friend of ours showed true Audrey Style when, after dating a wonderful man for about five months, he took her out to breakfast and said, "It's obvious we are perfect for one another, and in love with one another, and I would like us to live together for a year to see how things go . . ."

Almost before the words were even out of his mouth, she said (in the kindest way possible, of course), "No way."

Ever the deal maker (because he did not want to lose her), he said, "Well, what were you thinking?"

"I'll live with you for one month, that's long enough to see what's going on."

Now, we don't know if it is related—but she moved in, and two weeks later they were engaged.

In her own life, Audrey never encountered this situation, as men met her, fell in love with her, and wanted to marry her almost immediately. ("I was never engaged, just married," she once said wistfully of her romance with Mel Ferrer; and with her second husband, Dr. Andrea Dotti, she had a three-week engagement, marrying just six weeks after her divorce from Ferrer was final.)

The Goodbye Girl: Exit gracefully.

From the workplace to dating to the final day on a film set, Audrey knew that how you end a relationship is almost as important as how you begin—and says quite a bit about you.

We see this as AH ended (somewhat regretfully) her engagement to James Hanson. After *Gigi* and *Roman Holiday*, her life just kept speeding up. She had half a day off between the close of the Broadway show and having to pack and leave for Rome to start the picture. She loved James and wanted to get married . . . it just seemed that there wasn't any time. She was in New York, or L.A., then Rome, and now back on the road with *Gigi*. And her fiancé was still back in London. As she told Anita Loos, "When I found I couldn't find time to attend to the furnishing of our London flat, I suddenly knew I'd make a pretty bad wife. I would forever have to be studying parts, fitting costumes, and giving interviews. And what a humiliating spot to put a husband in . . . making him stand by, holding my coat, while I signed autographs for bobbie soxers!"

After *Roman Holiday* finished shooting, she and James had a conversation. According to Hanson, Audrey said, "I really don't think I want to get married at this time. I hate to do this to you. I love your family. . . ." James took it like a gentleman, and remembered, "There was disappointment, yes. But there was no rift or rupture, just a natural decision made by both sides."[9]

They were still so friendly that they continued to see each other when they could. At Christmas, Hanson flew to Chicago and spent the holiday with her. As Hanson recalled, "We spent a happy Christmas in Chicago, after which we parted as good friends."

Perhaps the early exit of her father and the trauma of World War II made Audrey extra sensitive to endings. Perhaps because she was so sensitive to hurts, she was even more careful with others' feelings, but if Audrey broke up with you, she let you down easy. And with one notable exception (meanie Mel Ferrer, which we will get to later), Audrey cherished her friendships and nurtured them her entire life. You might no longer be making a film together, or be the main man in her life, but once she revealed her heart to you, you were on Team Audrey forever.

---

[9] AH and Hanson always spoke positively of each other. In 1959, he married Geraldine Kaelin and had three children. JH went on to found a powerful industrial conglomerate worth $17 billion with interests ranging from tobacco to chemicals. In 1983, he was named a baron and admitted to the House of Lords. Years later, he and his wife ran into AH and Rob at an event, and AH said, "Well, now, we haven't done too badly for ourselves, have we?" Hanson died in 2004 at the age of eighty-two.

The "what might have been" factor. With use of your newfound *WWAD?* knowledge, this will be the prevailing sentiment among old admirers (who will, of course, be half in love with you forever after you so gracefully let them off the hook). The inherent wistfulness (mostly on their part, natch) of the situation is why you want to be a cool Audrey chick when ending things, and not the scary, quasi-stalker ex-girlfriend type.

This sentiment also gives rise to endless country music songs, a rather romantic ennui, one heck of a backstory, lack of appetite, and prominent cheekbones (all positives in the dating world, by the way), that final scene in *Casablanca*. . . .

An additional upside of your behaving so proactively is that he will invariably miss you for the rest of his life, because he will never see you in a ratty bathrobe in the morning, bitching about "Why didn't you go out and get milk?" You will never argue about whose turn it is to take out the garbage (his, always). He might not even have seen you wearing eyeglasses instead of contacts.

This glowy, romantic haze has no basis in reality, of course. But what the heck—sometimes it's cooler to walk, and be seen through the prism of the one that got away. God knows, this is what Audrey did with James Hanson, and with Bill Holden. Decades after they parted, Holden was being interviewed on television. "Who was the love of your life?" the host wanted to know.

Bill got a soft look in his eye, forgetting, for a moment, that a camera was on him. "Audrey," he said finally. "Audrey."

If all else fails, hit "Delete." But having said all this, there is one specific instance where Audrey was so hurt, so betrayed about what happened to her that she simply cut the man out of her life. And that is with Mel Ferrer.

During her fourteen-year marriage to Mel, Audrey put up with a lot—perhaps because of their son, Sean, born in 1960, perhaps because of society at the time. Mel, even to those who liked him, was a handful. "Mel was a strange guy," recalled Dominick Dunne. "I mean, I liked him . . . but he used to be so *grumpy*, he was a grumpy man!"

"Mel was a pain in the ass," says photographer Bob Willoughby, who remembers him endlessly fussing with Audrey on film sets and slowing things down.

Even their son, Sean, in his memoir, *Audrey Hepburn, An Elegant Spirit*, felt that Audrey stayed in the relationship longer than she should have for her own good.

But once she and Mel divorced in 1968, that was it: Mel was crossed off the list forever.

Audrey did not see him or speak to him until they saw each other again during Sean's first wedding ceremony in 1985. Mel had wanted to have the first dance with her but she refused, believing, quite rightly, that she and Rob should share that honor.

Touché.

MEETING AUDREY, MEETING MEL, MEETING MOM

Cecil Beaton, compulsive diarist and the future costume designer for *My Fair Lady*, first met Audrey and her mother at their flat in Mayfair on July 23, 1954. They had moved to London in 1948 after the war, to try to improve Audrey's chances of becoming a ballerina. While Audrey moved from ballet to the occasional modeling stint to appearing in the chorus of West End musicals, her mother supported them both by working as a manicurist, in a florist shop, and finally as manager of 65 South Audley Street in Mayfair, an ideal situation as it gave them both a place to live.

It was here that Beaton met them.

Beaton was an English dandy of the old school, a Victorian aesthete who wore his suits one size smaller because he thought it flattering. He loved the British royal family beyond all measure and was secretly, caustically bitchy toward practically every public figure who had the misfortune to cross his path.

He once famously, terribly, described "the other Hepburn"— Katharine—as "the egomaniac of all time . . . a raddled, rash-ridden, freckled, burnt, mottled, bleached and wizened piece of decaying matter. It is unbelievable, incredible that she can be exhibited in public." And this was while they were working together (quite successfully, she thought) on her 1969 Broadway hit, *Coco*. "She is a dried up boot," he decided.

On the other hand—and thank goodness for us—Beaton *loved* Audrey.

He had heard from Anita Loos what a delightful creature she was, "how full of talent." He knew that she had recently been given the leading part in a film called *Roman Holiday*, which, he was convinced, "will bring her at the top of her profession."

The night of Audrey's party, Beaton did not miss a thing. "If there were a safety pin, he'd find it," Andy Warhol said of him.

He was the first to arrive at Miss Hepburn's flat. "I spoke to the mother, Baroness Heemstra, a lady with a rather charming rolling accent, who told me that her daughter was dressing, was always late. Wouldn't I have some hors d'oeuvre, a martini? The guests, like all film people on social occasions, were unconsciously late. Mel Ferrer arrived, a charming, gangling man . . . who, no doubt as a result of his theatrical career, has developed a slightly professional charm of manner. He described A.H. to me as 'the biggest thing to come down the turnpike.'"

Energetic, addicted to deals and the telephone, both full of himself and a bit of a user in that modern American way (and not particularly kind to those who could not further his aims), Mel was the *anti*-Audrey—the kind of man who attended an Ivy League school and never let you forget it. Needless to say, Mr. Ferrer was never as universally loved as his future (fourth) bride.

The Dating Game

Match the beau Audrey was dating to the
film she was making at the time ...

1. *Two for the Road*	**A.** James Hanson
2. *My Fair Lady*	**B.** Mel Ferrer
3. *Bloodline*	**C.** Bill Holden
4. *Sabrina*	**D.** Albert Finney
5. *Roman Holiday*	**E.** Ben Gazzara
6. *Breakfast at Tiffany's*	**F.** George Clooney
7. *War and Peace*	**G.** Gregory Peck

CORRECT ANSWERS:

1. D—Albert Finney; 2. B—Mel Ferrer (verge of divorcing, during); 3. E—Ben Gazzara . . . Ben *Gazzara;* 4. C—Bill Holden, B—Mel Ferrer (on back burner); 5. A—James Hanson, G-Gregory Peck (rumored, untrue); 6. B—Mel Ferrer (unsupportive of project); 7. B—Mel Ferrer

Audrey appeared. "A new type of beauty," assessed Beaton, "huge mouth, flat Mongolian features, heavily painted eyes, a coconut coiffure, long nails without varnish, a wonderfully lithe figure, a long neck . . ." Still, it was Audrey's possible fame that fascinated Beaton. "A.H.'s enormous potential cinema success, with attendant salary, seems to have made little impression on this delightful human being. She appears to take wholesale adulation with a pinch of salt: gratitude rather than puffed-up pride. Everything very simple about and around her: no maid to help her dress, or to answer the door to the guests. . . ."

Not surprisingly, Beaton found himself attracted to her. "In a flash, I discovered A.H. chock-a-block with spritelike charm, and she has a sort of waifish, poignant sympathy. Without any of the preliminaries I felt that she cut through to a basic understanding that makes people friends. Nothing had to be explained: we liked one another."

THE AH RULES

Forget being a Rules Girl. Instead, opt for something much hipper and be an Audrey Girl.

Date like Audrey. Until there is an engagement, a ring on your finger, or a very serious conversation about where the two of you are going (initiated by him, of course), keep your options open and keep dating. Don't act like you are the wife until you actually are the wife (if this is what you want). You're busy. You have a life, *Bill Holden's on line two*. The worst thing you can do is put your life on hold, waiting for him to get his act together.

Let's say you would like to get married—something that was definitely important to Audrey. Now, Audrey never had the problem of the man in her life not asking her to marry him, because frankly, every guy who met her wanted to marry her. Immediately. But back here in the real world, there are definitely some Audrey-inspired game plans to help us out.

Don't talk about yourself . . . except perhaps in the mildest way. Boring! Audrey's upbringing was almost Victorian in that it was considered bad form to be too showy. In today's transparent Internet culture, if someone really wants to find out about you, short of your credit report and the interest rate on your mortgage—and heck, they can probably figure out that, too—they will.

Flirt like hell. It's good practice, and it makes the day go faster. Plus, it never hurts to have the butcher (the waiter, the guy who makes your cappuccino in the morning) on your side. It also keeps your energy up and moving in the right direction. Whether you're waiting in line at the Motor Vehicles Department, or running errands on a Saturday morning, it makes life more entertaining.

Aim high. Face it, any woman who had Gregory Peck, Hubert de Givenchy, Ralph Lauren, Nancy Reagan, Albert Finney, Richard Avedon, Kevin Aucoin, Steven Meisel, Sean Connery, Roger Moore, David Niven, Cary Grant, Fred Astaire, Gary Cooper, William Holden, Isaac Mizrahi, Michael Kors, Rosemary Clooney, Jeffrey Banks, Steven Spielberg, William Wyler, Peter O'Toole, Stanley Donen, and Bill Clinton as admirers must have been doing something right. If you are going to get in the game, by all means—don't sell yourself short in the romance or friendship department. You deserve the best.

Keep a clear head. As an Audrey Gal, you do not date one person for years (and years and years), waiting for him to make up his mind.[10] Look at your romantic situation realistically. With today's loosened societal structures, you can tell in a few weeks (or even sooner) if someone is the right person for you.

And listen to people—when someone tells you something, such as, "I want to get married (someday), I just don't want to get married now,"[11] believe him. Then make the decision that is best for you.

This will save you a lot of heartache in the long run.

Don't dumb yourself down. AH never had to act like a dumb blonde, because, frankly, she wasn't. If some guy is intimidated by your essential Audrey-esque fabulousness, then you don't want him in your life, anyway, because the entire point of having a personal relationship is to encourage each other and raise your standards as high as you can.

R-E-S-P-E-C-T. Otis and Aretha knew what they were talking about when they said "respect yourself." If you are dating someone who is not treating you properly, go to Washington and have dinner with that cute senator from Massachusetts. If you are married and your husband insists on continuing to date, dump him. In other words, don't be a doormat, and don't make yourself too available.

Keep the real estate. Don't give up your apartment or home to live with a guy, and if possible, keep your former residence in your own name, in case something happens (ahem) in the future. If all goes well, you can always pass it on to your children, or nieces or nephews in years to come. Audrey bought La Paisible, her home in Switzerland, in 1965, and kept the house through both of her marriages and her long-term relationship with Robert Wolders.

---

[10] Unless you want to, of course.

[11] Translation: He does not want to marry *you*.

Have your own gig. AH was a working woman her entire life, and although she was married for a time, she was largely in charge of the care of her two sons and her mother, and she also helped out her father. Which leads to . . .

Have your own money. Whether you have a job, work for it, or have your own inheritance . . . money is freedom.

Include him in your life and your activities. That is, once you have been involved with someone, and trust the situation. For example, if you've just won an Oscar and a Tony, and are currently starring in a Broadway show (as AH did with Mel in *Ondine*) and are dating an actor, do him, and yourself, a favor: Bring him on as your costar. The critics and producers might cry, "Machiavellian!"[12] but hey, at least you'll be able to spend time together, and it will give you something to do on the weekends when you can study your lines together.

Disappear for a while. After you've closed that hit on Broadway (or whatever), don't be afraid to go to Switzerland and rest for a while by yourself, as AH did after a three-month run starring in *Ondine* on Broadway in 1954. Mel chased her halfway around the world and begged her to marry him.

For men, absence really does make the heart grow fonder.

Never underestimate the power of the grand gesture. Once things are settled and you decide to marry, all bets are off—or on (as it were). In August 1954, for his thirty-seventh birthday, Audrey sent Mel a platinum Rolex watch with "Mad About the Boy" (they both loved Cole Porter) engraved on the back. Mel took this as a sign that Audrey was ready to commit to him. He flew to Switzerland where she was vacationing and formally proposed. And she formally accepted.

---

[12] Or worse—as director Alfred Lunt and the critics noted—the male lead can't act.

Movie Magic

Of course, part of the reason we think people fell in love more quickly in the old days was that they had better dialogue. Here are Audrey Hepburn (as Reggie Lampert) and Cary Grant (as Peter Joshua) in *Charade*, meeting at the ski resort of Chalet du Mont d'Arbois in Mageve, Switzerland. Audrey is stunningly dressed in a Givenchy ski ensemble, and Cary Grant is, well, Cary Grant. Needless to say, they are both Euro cool.

CG
Do we know each other?

AH
Why, do you think we're going to?

CG
(annoyed)
I don't know—how would I know?

AH
Because I know an awful lot of
people and until one of them dies,
I couldn't possibly meet anyone
else.

CG
Well, if anyone goes on the
critical list, let me know.

AH
(coolly)
Quitter.

THE AUDREY/GEORGE CLOONEY CONNECTION

Rosemary Clooney, the great American song stylist (and aunt of George), also knew Audrey and Mel in 1953, when Audrey first came to Hollywood. Seated on a couch at a small party at the River House in New York City thirty-five years later, she tells her own Audrey story.

"Audrey and I knew each other at Paramount—our dressing rooms were next to each other." Rosemary smiles, remembering. "She was lovely!

"I was married to José Ferrer[13] at the time and one night I invited her home for dinner—it was just the two of us, and after dinner we were sitting, watching television, I think, and she asked me, 'What do you think of Mel Ferrer?' And I said: 'Oh my god, he's the worst— he'd walk over anyone who got in his way, he steamrolls women to get what he wants, he's terrible. . . .'

"She didn't say much, just 'hmmmmmmmmmmm.'

"Later, after she'd left, I spoke to José and said, 'I think I said something that maybe I shouldn't have—'

"And he said, 'What's that?'

"'Well, I had dinner with Audrey—she asked what I thought of Mel, and I told her.'

"José said, 'Big mistake.'

"'Why?'

"'She's dating him!'

"'*What!*'

"'You didn't know that?'

"'Why didn't you tell me?'

---

[13] To further confuse matters—no relation to Mel.

" 'Everyone knows!'

" 'Nobody told *me!*'

Telling the story in 1999, Rosemary gave a great laugh—well, what can you do, it was a while ago, and now, what the heck, it's a great anecdote. And what happened at the end? "Audrey and I later joked about it and she eventually forgave me," recalled Clooney.

But no matter what outsiders thought of the match (and who knows, really, what goes on between two people, because clearly, in the beginning they loved each other), Audrey Hepburn and Mel Ferrer were married in a civil ceremony at Buochs, Switzerland, in the parlor of the local mayor's house on September 24, 1954. The next day, they repeated their vows at a religious ceremony in a thirteenth-century chapel in Bürgenstock. Audrey wore a lyrical Pierre Balmain dress with a crown of white roses, looking as hopeful and impossibly beautiful as any bride.

Her mother wept through the entire ceremony.

PLAN B:
IF HE HAS NO INTEREST IN SAYING, "I DO"

If, on the other hand, he does not want to make the ultimate ~~sacrifice~~, we mean commitment, you have a few decisions to make. And, of course, Audrey is here to help you make sure they are good ones.

Be the decider. If your ultimate goal is to get married, make a clear decision: Either marry the guy or break it off and move on, as Audrey did with James Hanson, Bill Holden, and JFK.

Don't be the eternal girlfriend. You know the one, the slightly woebegone girl who hangs around forever—decorating his apartment, buying the sheets he is too busy too buy, cooking elaborate (with many, many hard-to-find ingredients) four-course dinners for him every night, and not asking too many questions about what the future might bring. And waiting, waiting for him to pop the question.

The Eternal GF might get mad, she might sulk, she might complain to her girlfriends or mother about how he "needs more time" and "isn't ready" to make a real commitment just yet. But still, like Penelope at her loom in the tower, waiting for cunning Odysseus, she waits. And waits. And waits.

Please.

Whatever your age. Whatever life experiences brought you to a place where you think it is okay to hang around and wait for scraps (or, worse, that this is the way it is supposed to be), listen to us, and if you're not going to listen to us, listen to Audrey: Don't Be That Woman.

If a man wants to be with you—wants to marry you, perhaps raise children together, hang out in the South of France, wake up next to you every day for the rest of his life, bring you coffee in bed—he is going to close the deal *pronto* (as Andrea Dotti would have put it). And no amount of love, will, desire, or "hanging in there" on your part is going to make it happen.

Dating is not like a *Law & Order* episode, where possession is nine-tenths of the law, because frankly, you could cook dinner for him, clean his car, and pick up his dry cleaning for the rest of your life and still not get what you want.

And whatever you do—don't fall into the trap of moving in with the guy, believing that this will invariably lead to a walk down the aisle, which is why Audrey never did anything like this when she wanted to get married. Don't be half-assed. And trust us: Men respect power (in themselves and others). Treat yourself with the respect you deserve, and the guy you are with will, too.

Don't demean yourself by hanging around forever. Asking "When are we going to get married?" is as pointless as asking "Do you love me?" or worse, "Does this make me look fat?" When you've reached the point where you are asking those questions, it is clearly time to shake the whole thing up with your Holly Golightly–inspired consciousness. So go to Rome for the summer and shoot a movie, get your hair cut, sell your screenplay for a nice six-figure sum, buy those Manolos you've been coveting, rent a convertible, and drive up the coast (say, to Maine).

There is just *no way* Audrey would hang around waiting for some guy to make up his mind. In 1953, while AH was in San Francisco with the road tour of *Gigi*, columnist Dorothy Kilgallen asked if she'd "always had this many beaus buzzing around her." She replied, "Well, I'll say this—I've never wanted for one—not since I was seventeen, anyway."

Take his name. No matter how liberated or evolved your man (says he) is, remember: Every man secretly wants his wife to have his surname. It's a pride thing.

If you are an author or world-famous actress, you might have to keep your name professionally, but in your private life, take his. While Audrey may have been "Audrey Hepburn" above the credits, she was proudly "Audrey Hepburn Ferrer" or "AHF" (or later, S. Dotti) in her personal life.

Sometimes, you just have to laugh at 'em. After Audrey broke up with Holden, he promptly went on an extended world tour and tried to forget her by seducing a different woman in every country. Which he pretty much managed to do. Back in Hollywood he told AH the story, perhaps to make her jealous, but her response was to laugh and say, "Oh, *Bill* . . ."

Be a riddle wrapped up in an enigma. Keep them guessing about your personal life. When AH shot *Roman Holiday*, the gossips were awash in stories that she and Gregory Peck were having a romance. In fact, he had just met the woman who would become his second wife (the journalist Veronique Passani). Knowing the real story, Audrey and Greg had a lot of laughs about this.

Behave well. Be gracious and remember: Real life (like Hollywood) is a lot like high school — everybody talks!

Be yourself. Dating is really the perfect time to get out in the world, learn what you like, negotiate what works for you, and, quite frankly, have fun. Having said this, the best way is to just be relaxed and be yourself. Easier said than done, perhaps, but just think of how much people will like you when they see your real personality.

Enthusiasm — not coolness — is cool. Audrey had enthusiasm in spades. Dominick Dunne's first memory of her is at a dinner party at Gary Cooper's when she first arrived in Hollywood.

"Rocky Cooper ran a *fabulous* house . . . ," he recalled. "This was when people made an effort, when women wore jewelry to dinner. . . ." He didn't know her then but she was seated down the table from him, and Billy Wilder had just said something that made her laugh. "Oh, she had a great laugh," Dunne recalls. "Such a great laugh from such a tiny woman. I loved it."

So if you feel strongly about something — a joke you just heard, the latest Simpsons movie, the Republican Party — let people know.

Keep the faith. And finally, this is probably the most important Audrey-esque attribute to take to heart. At the risk of possibly belittling the importance of your personal life, this will serve you well not only in socializing, but at work, in life, *everything* — and that is: Have faith.

No matter what happens — never lose sight of what you want and also of the belief that it will (somehow) all work out in the end. As Martin Luther King, Jr., said, "The ultimate measure of a man is not where he stands in moments of comfort and convenience, but where he stands at times of challenge and controversy."

So wherever you stand in your life right now—and believe us, there may be some dark days someday—keep going, keep going. As Audrey did.

And look at it this way: If nothing else, you will have some great stories to tell your grandchildren.

How to Meet (Movie Star) Cute

You've seen it in the movies. Stars are always meeting and falling in love in the most opportune ways—at a bookstore, in an elevator, on the *Titanic* while it is sinking. . . . It's terrific. Here are some Audrey Ways to meet your own leading man (or lady).

Meet at work.

Face it, Hollywood is one giant dating pool, with the best-looking people in the world meeting on movie sets, at the gym, Pink's hot dog stand, the craft services table. Not only is there is a lot of downtime to hang out and socialize, but people are often paid (a *lot*) to get thrown into inherently romantic situations to see what develops.

Frankly, we think this is fabulous!

Why don't you mimic this? Recent studies say that more than 43% of people meet their spouse/significant other at the office . . . because this is where people are spending 93% of their waking hours, anyway, so why not?

Don't overlook the nice guy.

AH admitted herself that she barely would have given Rob W. a second look when she was younger, but in her Third Act, this kind, gentlemanly, and, quite frankly, *très* handsome man was Audrey's beau ideal. After years of disappointment, here, finally, was a man who had her best interests at heart.

And still does.

Become famous.

How you accomplish this is up to you, but we think it is best to do this on the strength of your accomplishments, rather than infamy. Think Charles A. Lindbergh or Jonas Salk rather than O. J. Simpson. So whatever you're doing, try to be the absolute best you can be. Right out of the box, Audrey was a star—above-the-title billing, an Oscar, an Emmy, and the cover of *Time* magazine, all within the same year. We're not saying it's fair, we're just saying it's true. So whether it be inventing the Internet, collecting comic books, or writing a column for the local newspaper, become obsessed with something you are really good at, and raise your profile accordingly, because famous people get lots more dates than the non-famous.

Let friends fix you up.

The old reliable is still the best way to meet people. In fact, Audrey met both her husbands and Rob Wolders through friends introducing them.

SEX APPEAL = THE .7 SOLUTION

What do Audrey Hepburn, Kate Moss, Twiggy, Sophia Loren, Marilyn Monroe, Liz Taylor, Raquel Welch, and even Elle "The Body" Macpherson have in common? Their waist-to-hip ratio is .7.

Let us explain. According to Dr. Devendra Singh, a psychologist at the University of Texas at Austin, who has spent the past twenty-five years studying the correlation between body shape, health, and perceptions of beauty, all of these women—in addition to being legendary beauties—have one thing in common: Their waists are noticeably narrower than their hips.

In scientific terms, this is known as WHR—the waist-hip ratio—and, according to Dr. Singh, this very scientific ratio is what makes men find certain women attractive. For everyone who failed in biology, the hourglass curves of a woman (along with clear skin, bright eyes, and glossy hair) signify fertility, and men are biologically programmed to act accordingly. "Basically," says Dr. Singh, "a man wants a woman who is strong, who is healthy, and can bear healthy children and be able to raise them."

In a 1995 study, Dr. Singh studied males from Africa, the Azores, Hong Kong, India, the Netherlands, and the United States. Volunteers were given a selection of photographs of females of different shapes and sizes and asked to rank them in terms of physical beauty. "They all selected the same women," Dr. Singh says, somewhat amazed. "They all seemed to like women with a low waist-to-hip ratio. We also wanted to see how early it starts. In America and India, eight-year-old boys selected the same women as the grown-ups. They looked at the women and said, 'That's the one that's beautiful.'" Dr. Singh compares this low-WHR instinct with people's innate love of sugar: "You don't have to teach a kid to like chocolate," he observes.

Totally un-PC, but probably true.

• • •

So here's the deal with the .7 solution—are you optimistic enough to find out yours? To determine the ratio, divide your waist measurement (in either inches or centimeters) by your hip measurement. Ideally, you want something in the .7 to .9 range. And putting aside for a moment your secret dream of looking like a Marc Jacobs model, there is a medical reason for keeping an eye on this measurement. Research shows that people with "apple-shaped" bodies (with more weight around the waist) face more health risks such as diabetes or heart disease than those with "pear-shaped" bodies who carry more weight around the hips.

And what does this "belle" curve have to do with Audrey—who did not carry much weight at either her waist or her hips? If her dress form at Givenchy's atelier is to be believed—and god knows, we think it is—Audrey maintained an impressive 31½"-22"-31½" her entire life. But at the end of the day (spoken like a true man), Dr. Singh says that "in spite of all these scientific commonalities, beauty is still a mystery."[14]

WOULD AUDREY . . .

Ask a guy out first? That would be a *no*. Without even intending to, Audrey was probably one of the first (as were most of the women in the 1950s) Rules Girls.

Offer to pay on a date? See above.

---

[14] For the record, Dr. Singh's favorite Audrey movie is *Charade*. "And what was that one, with Peter O'Toole, where they try to steal the artwork? [*How to Steal a Million*] She was so charming in that."

Try Internet dating?

Okay, for starters, she is Audrey Hepburn, and half the women on the site are probably using the term "Audrey-esque" to describe themselves. To say nothing of all the Audrey fan sites that she would no doubt be a little freaked out by.

Keep her (romantic) cards close to her chest?

Yes. Audrey had her share of love affairs, but did we know about them? No. "She had her romances," observed Bob Willoughby, "but nobody really knew it at the time." When it came to her love life, Audrey knew enough to keep 'em guessing.

Hesitate to ask a fiancé for business advice?

No. In fact, James Hanson was very helpful when AH was just starting out. Signed to a restrictive contract with a British studio, as an old friend of Lew Wasserman's of MCA, Hanson was able to "put in his two cents' worth" to improve her contract with Paramount. And he did.

Believe in love at first sight?

Yes. Audrey met her second husband, Dr. Andrea Dotti, at a Mediterranean cruise hosted by Princess Olimpia Torlonia and her industrialist husband, Paul-Louis Weiller. Andrea was an assistant professor at the University of Rome. Handsome, witty, charming, and nine years Audrey's junior, he quickly became smitten. He said that he and Audrey fell in love "somewhere between Ephesus and Athens. It was not that she came to cry on my shoulder about the breakup of her marriage. . . . We were playmates on a cruise ship with other friends, and slowly, day by day, our relationship grew into what it is."

For her part, Audrey said, "Do you know what it's like when a brick falls on your head? That's how my feelings for Andrea first hit me. It just happened out of the blue. He was such an enthusiastic, cheerful person [and] as I got to know him, I found he was also a thinking, very deep feeling person."

chapter 3

Zen Audrey

"I think the most compelling thing
about her was that she was so present.
That's a lesson for us all." –Kevin Aucoin

Audrey Hepburn was cool.

And not because she was beautiful, or had Givenchy designing for her, or that her day job was as a
world-famous actress. In fact, it could be argued that
Audrey was a world-famous actress, and cool, and
possibly even beautiful, *because* of everything going on
within her—the Audrey that few people, save her
family and close friends, got to see.

In this chapter, we explore Audrey's interior life,
and the not so obvious things that made her so
compelling—her discipline, her intelligence, her
generosity (as Diana Vreeland said, "Some people give
in this world and some people take. . . ."). But coupled
with her extremely public life, there is also her
shyness, her privacy, and her need for solitude.

Audrey's emotional core was interesting because she was both vulnerable and exceptionally strong. This vulnerability is what made her such a compelling actress—you see her on the screen, and you know exactly what she is feeling. But she was also—and please excuse the very non-AH expression—within her femininity and her grace: strong as hell.

And it is this tension (we think) that makes Audrey such a remarkable person to watch. Cathleen Nesbitt, who was assigned by the producers of *Gigi* to take Hepburn under her wing when she first appeared on Broadway, thought Audrey did not "have much idea of phrasing. She had no idea how to project, and she would come bounding onto the stage like a gazelle. But she had that rare thing— audience authority, the thing that makes everybody look up at you when you are on stage."

Finally, we recognize the importance of having an interior life. For it is only by studying the many facets of Audrey's experience that we can learn to cultivate our own interests—whatever they might be—and elevate our own experience.

• • •

"Beauty is not caused," wrote Emily Dickinson. "It is." Audrey's beauty was based not only on her physical attributes (which were considerable), but her interior self. Part of it was her history. You might not know much about her, but you just knew from looking at her—even when we first saw her in *Roman Holiday* at the age of twenty-four—this is a woman who has had a very interesting life.

Most if it came from within—her intelligence, her humor, her vulnerability, all that was asked of her. She carried it all on her slim, straight shoulders: the absence of her father, advancing her mother's hopes, the hunger of her adolescence, the loss, the secrets, the uncer- tainty. As well as the need for beauty. For peace. Some kind of grace.

And like all great actors she had a need—*love me*. Love me, and I will put myself before you. I will show myself on screen, in photographs. You will never know me, of course, not the real me, but you will know the dream of me. The dream I choose to present to you — that better version of yourself you wish to become.

And then I will disappear. Like all great artists, I know the power of the final act, and the resilience of the human heart.

But whether it was her looks, her intelligence, or the tone of her voice — whatever alchemy combined to make Audrey Hepburn the memorable person she was is almost beside the point. Because the fact remained, if you met Audrey, there was a very good chance that you would never forget it.

Director Billy Wilder knew this. At a tribute at Lincoln Center in 1991, he recalled that "the first picture I made with Audrey was *Sabrina*, and I very vividly remember the very first day, the very first scene, actually. You looked around and suddenly there was this dazzling creature looking like a wide-eyed deer prancing through the forest, and it took exactly five minutes for everybody to fall in love with her — the cameramen, the other actors, the extras, the electricians, and yours truly also."

But unlike most stars of her caliber (or, let's be honest, lesser caliber or no caliber at all), Audrey was not a vast vortex of egomania and take, take, take, take, take. She gave. As a friend, she had a tremendous capacity to give love. And once she trusted you, that was it.

Connie Wald, the widow of well-known Hollywood producer Jerry Wald and a dear friend of Audrey's, was asked: What was it like to have her as a friend?

"It was like the rest of her life, she was thoughtful and loving and full of care. I remember one Easter, she arrived here, and she had this huge box from a great chocolatier in Lausanne, and the box of little eggs, the most beautiful thing, and she lugged it all the way from Switzerland! And flowers, and letters . . .

"She was just, as they say, the perfect friend. We would always laugh at people and situations and carry on. Private jokes. She had a delicious sense of humor."

But the emotional accessibility that made her such a great friend or artist—can anyone forget the look in her eyes in *Roman Holiday* when she and Gregory Peck realize they are never going to see each other again?—also made her more sensitive to the slights and barbs that make up living. According to Rob, "once she sensed that she could trust somebody, she'd do anything for them. And if she were disappointed in them, it would be the end of the world for her. She suffered more than most of us."

Audrey herself was not unaware of this emotional tendency in herself, admitting to Larry King that "it always boils down to the enormous need of not only receiving love, but an enormous *need* to give it! It is true that I had an extraordinary mother. She herself was not a very affectionate person in the sense that I today consider affection. I spent a lot of time looking for it, I found it. She's a fabulous mother, but she came from another era, she was born in 1900, Victorian influence still. Of great discipline, of great ethics. Lots of love within her, not always able to show it. And very strict."

But when Audrey was with animals or children, there were no expectations, no need to perform. They didn't want anything from her. She could just be herself in the same way that animals and children just "are." And in them, Audrey sensed a vulnerability—on some level, they needed her—that allowed her to open her heart.

POSSIBLE EMOTIONAL UPHEAVAL SITUATION #1: WHEN THE CARDS FALL IN YOUR FAVOR

It is one thing to stay humble when you are slinging coffee at Starbucks (heck, it's practically a requirement), but in true Audrey fashion, you are going to be a huge success at whatever endeavor you undertake—and then what? Herewith, following AH's life lessons, our advice.

| Stay Centered |

And so we have the question: What happens *after* success? As screenwriter Albert Goldman observed, "No man is really changed by success. What happens is that success works on the man's personality like a truth drug, bringing him out of the closet and revealing . . . what was always inside his head."

| Check Your Ego at the Door |

In Audrey's case, we have spoken to dozens of people who knew her—as a friend, on movie sets, during photo shoots, even during the UNICEF trips, and never, never, never did she show one iota of star 'tude.

(Now, Mel . . . on the other hand, was Mr. Attitude. Years ago in New York—and we are admitting up front, this is a *terrible* story, but wonderful, too, because it reveals character—Dominick Dunne had a secretary who was Mel's personal secretary before working for Dunne. She had run errands for Mr. Ferrer and he owed her some petty cash. He paid her in stamps.

Not food stamps. Not S & H stamps.

"*Postage* stamps!" Dunne practically crows as he tells this story, nearly fifty years later. "Audrey never would have done that!")

Instead, we have stories of Audrey bringing homemade brownies to the set of *The Children's Hour* (and Shirley MacLaine rhapsodizing over the "powdered sugar sprinkled on top"). Buying Rob a puppy for his fiftieth birthday, because he had never had a dog before. Leaving a message on famed hairstylist Garren's home machine, after he had done her hair for a *Vanity Fair* shoot with Steven Meisel. "Hello, this is Audrey Hepburn, I'm not sure if you remember me. . . ." (And don't worry, Garren saved the tape.)

| Don't Lose Yourself |

Audrey may have looked like a princess, but she rose to the top—and stayed there—of one of the most brutal, cutthroat, and demanding professions in the world. Part of her success as a person (and, truth be told, as an actress) is that she knew who she was and, throughout her life, remained true to her essential nature. This proved enormously helpful as AH navigated the hothouse stratosphere where celebrities and, in particular, Oscar-winning actresses can basically get away with anything they want—and then parlay that into a) an *OK!* magazine cover story with photo, writer, and text approval and b) a career resurgence.

| Cultivate Other Interests |

Audrey loved music, and loved to dance. In her free time off the set, she listened to jazz and was known to lug her LPs to whatever house or hotel she was renting. She also had a very good ear and spoke four languages. She had many loves—small dogs, couture, William Holden (for a time), and the occasional Scotch.

She also loved to read—fiction, poetry. In later years, UNICEF photographer John Isaac was stunned when she recited his favorite poet, Rumi, back to him.

| Remain Low-Key |

You are one of the most famous personalities of your time, and yet you are also one of the nicest, kindest, and most memorable to work with. . . . We can't give you any advice how to pull off this tightrope walk, but do it. For psychic, emotional, and just generally good karma (as well as all of the positive things your friends will say about you behind your back), be as talented, low-key, generous, and inherently cool as you possibly can. Think Elvis Presley. Think George Clooney. Think Meryl Streep. Has anyone ever had a bad thing to say about them?

It's worth it.

| Get Over Yourself |

As a world-famous actress, AH could have run roughshod over anyone in her path (see: Elizabeth Taylor in her heyday). Instead, she revealed her inherent style by extending herself to others. In 1976, she told *People* magazine, "I don't think you have to make just the big gestures to be helpful. Every second of every day you can do something. Just a cheerful smile does wonders for a beginning."

| Remember What Mom (Really) Thought of You |

If you are an international superstar trying to keep your feet on the ground, it helps to have a mother who is somewhat dismissive of your talent (at least to you), so that you don't get a swelled head. By all reports, Audrey's mother was old-style: a "stiff upper lip," somewhat Victorian woman—she had to have been, to survive the Nazis in 1943—and Audrey definitely suffered from her emotional remove.

There is also her jaw-dropping quote in regard to her well-known daughter: "Isn't it remarkable how far you've gotten considering how little talent you have?"

In the excessively child-centric era we live in today, even we have to say: *Wow.*

"Pick a day. Enjoy it—to the hilt. The day as it comes. People as they come . . . the past, I think has helped me appreciate the present—and I don't want to spoil any of it by fretting about the future."–AH

POSSIBLE EMOTIONAL UPHEAVAL SITUATION #2: WHEN THINGS DON'T GO YOUR WAY

Now, we realize: It is easy to be Zen and groovy and accepting when the cards fall in your favor. But what happens when they don't?

For Audrey, one of her professional challenges came when she failed to be nominated for an Oscar in *My Fair Lady*. Hollywood, Jack Warner, and all of Audrey's friends were in an uproar. The press, always willing to stir up controversy, encouraged the media frenzy that followed when Julie Andrews (who originated the Eliza Doolittle role on Broadway but would not audition for the movie role, and hence was not officially offered it) was nominated for *Mary Poppins*.

The story has always been that AH was distraught and heartbroken that she was not nominated. That it was a huge deal for her.

In reality, Audrey was pretty accepting about the whole thing.

In an amazing (and newly unearthed) letter she wrote to director George Cukor on March 8, 1965, she laid out her thoughts about the whole brouhaha.

"As for the whole nomination mishmosh—I think I am the only one not in the dark," she writes. Everyone is searching for an "explanation," and it seems to Audrey that the whole thing is all very simple: "My performance was not up to snuff." Further, she goes on to assure Cukor that if people were out to get her, or Jack Warner, or if they wanted to "ensure Julie Andrews's Oscar, their sentiments would have automatically been cancelled out had my bravura been worthy."

She confides in Cukor that "because MY FAIR LADY meant so terribly much to me I had sort of secretly hoped for a nomination but never counted on the Oscar. Therefore disappointed I is but not astounded like my chums seem to be or a lot of the press for that matter.

"What does amaze me is the bullabaloo which ensued and the constant pressure which was brought about for almost a week to get me to come to California for the big night. . . ."

| Think! (Pink or Otherwise) |

Audrey used her brain. She considered things. According to Rob, "In my experience, Audrey was the most introspective person I have ever met, always trying to discover, self-discovery. On the other hand, she had an extraordinary ability to laugh, to try to enjoy life. So she would be very determined to get to the essence of an issue, which required study and application, but then afterwards, she had this tremendous need to laugh, to amuse. A great cut-up. She was always able to make fun of herself."

| Respect Yourself |

When she sang, "Respect Yourself," soul singer Mavis Staples knew what she was talking about, as (in her own way) did Audrey.

Bob Willoughby, who spent close to thirty years on the very incestuous atmosphere of film sets (part boot camp, part luxury to rival Louis XIV), has a very good observation about Audrey. "Hollywood is very gossipy, backbiting—it's worse than grade school! People in Hollywood always take potshots at one another, but with Audrey—never. I never saw or heard anything like that. And I think the clue is: Automatically, in her own way, she demanded respect."

| Develop a Sense of Privacy |

Audrey obviously had a lot going on, inside. This used to be called "European mystery." You could tell just by looking at her, Audrey had a very cool interior life—you just were not part of it. And yet, she was very emotionally open and vulnerable as a person, and as an actress. This is especially intriguing to us as Americans, since we tend to Let Everything Out, at all times.

| Make Time for "Me" Time |

Like all great stars—those whose luck or talent plucked them from obscurity—Audrey, Bob Willoughby thought, had "this dichotomy that you felt she was a good friend, and yet, you felt there was a distancing. Usually, if you see actors on the set and they are sitting out between takes, there is a tendency for the crew to sit and schmooze—I never see that with Audrey. There was some deference that the crew gave to her to give her the time alone."

Stanley Donen, who directed her in three movies[15] and who knew her as well as anyone, felt the same way. "[Audrey] had polished her personality until it didn't have a rough spot anywhere. But there was another, hidden part of her persona. With all of her manners, she kept me from getting totally intimate. So I longed to get closer, to get behind whatever was the invisible, but decidedly present barrier between her and the rest of us mere mortal human beings. Something, some unseen screen was there, holding me back from getting as close as I wanted. That barrier made her all the more desirable.

"I don't mean to imply that I thought she was playing a game with me. But she always kept a little part of herself in reserve, which was hers alone, and I couldn't ever find out what it was, let alone share it with her."

This solitude was part of Audrey's strength: Her secrets, her experience, even her celebrity drew us to her and kept us apart. This impossible unknowing, too, made us love her even more.

---

[15] *Funny Face* (1957), *Charade* (1963), *Two for the Road* (1967).

| Be Consistent |

But perhaps most importantly—as one of the most famous women in the world her entire adult life—here are some of the things Audrey *didn't* do: Develop an addiction to prescription drugs; become a spokesperson for the National Rifle Association; appear on QVC (although who knows—she might have, to raise money for UNICEF); appear on *Oprah*; become a Scientologist; live in a gated community; marry her trainer/bodyguard/backup dancer; own a G4 jet; get hospitalized for "exhaustion"; close down a movie set for bad behavior; date George Clooney; spend time in rehab; cry on a *Barbara Walters Special*; refer to herself in the third person; drive a Hummer; expose her belly button; have a child out of wedlock; get married in Vegas; give too much of herself away; visit the Playboy Mansion; appear on a reality television show; get a tattoo; befriend Michael Jackson; date a rock star; get breast implants; allow her home to be open for tours after her death; get paid to wear a designer's clothing; appear in *Us Weekly* magazine; write a tell-all memoir; expound her religious beliefs; be asked "What are you wearing?" at the Oscars by a reporter; hurt anyone's feelings; hire Max Clifford; get arrested for shoplifting; forget to say thank you; get arrested for drink-driving; be paraded in handcuffs by the police; appear on *David Letterman*; be a punch line for one of David Letterman's monologues; have embarrassing videos of herself show up on the Internet; do anything to embarrass herself—or us—ever.

Namaste, Baby . . .
Clip-and-Save Audrey Advice

This one's for the bathroom mirror—one of our favorite Audrey quotes. And, really, if you think about it, it is all about acceptance and gratitude. Two things we can *all* do well to keep in mind.

When the chips are down, when you are having a crummy day, week, year, keep this in mind, from our girl Audrey: "I decided, very early on, just to accept life unconditionally; I never expected it to do anything special for me, yet I seemed to accomplish far more than I had ever hoped. Most of the time it just happened to me without my ever seeking it."

HOW TO CULTIVATE
YOUR INNER AUDREY

| Turn It Off |

When she needed to recharge her energy, AH hightailed it out of Hollywood, or whatever film set she was on, and headed to Switzerland. Or Paris.

Your options do not need to be so dramatic (or costly). Instead, take a break from the television, newspapers, magazines, or endlessly scanning the Internet for the latest "news" (which is, generally, truth be told, bad news). Go for a walk, take a yoga class, meditate for an hour, sit on a park bench, and read for a while.

| Make the World Go Away |

In spite of your view of your own personal self-importance, you do not always need to be so accessible. When Charles de Gaulle was president of France, he would go to his country house for the weekend and holidays. If you wanted to reach him, you would call the guardhouse, they would write down the message, and an aide would walk it to the main house.

And de Gaulle would respond. Or not.

So it is not a bad thing to turn off the endless stream of modern media, and your BlackBerry, and the phone, and take a breather from it all. Your brain will thank you. And since stress plays havoc with your looks, your skin will thank you, too.

"The world is too much with us," said Wordsworth. And he was right.

| Throw Off the Traces Once in a While |

In the utterly believable *Roman Holiday*, Princess Audrey skips out on the royal gig and enjoys a day (and night) of freedom with the preternaturally handsome Gregory Peck. While we're not saying make a habit of it (there is, after all, no known evidence of Slacker Audrey), go ahead—call in sick, leave your BlackBerry home, hop on the back of that Vespa and go for a ride. Go to Paris and study cooking. When that Dick Avedon-esque photographer asks you to dance, say *yes*.

| Lose Your Inner Scrooge |

If you don't like (well, love) children, this is not very Audrey-esque, because it turns out that Audrey loved babies, children, and all animals (but particularly small dogs). So when you're on a plane in first class and a nearby toddler is having a meltdown, think of a way to help the situation rather than rolling your eyes and bitching to the stewardess.

| "The Hell with It" |

Perhaps it had something to do with the fear, or the unexpected violence she saw during World War II, but Audrey was very aware—at a very young age—of the random nature of life. In our most useful example of Zen Audrey, AH always did the best that she could, whatever her situation—her early ballet lessons, working on *Roman Holiday* or *My Fair Lady*, her marriages, raising her children—and then said: The hell with it, and let the chips fall where they may.

| Enjoy Your Own Company |

We're not saying you need to turn into Greta Garbo, but Audrey had no problem being alone. In fact, there were times she preferred it.

Once, a reporter asked, "Do you ever feel lonely?"

And she responded, "When the chips are down, you are alone. That's the kind of loneliness that is terrifying. Fortunately, I've always had a chum I could call. And I love to be alone. It doesn't bother me one bit. I'm my own company, though I wouldn't want to be alone because nobody loves me or cares for me. I can spend time happily alone because I know somebody is going to walk in the door. I'm rather cheerful by nature—it's my best defense against the aches on the inside."

In Case You Are Still Wondering– Why Bother with Your Interior Life?

Trust us: No matter how Audrey perceived, or presented, herself, she had it.

Bob Willoughby, the photographer who shot practically every star in the world during the glory days of Hollywood—Marilyn Monroe, Elizabeth Taylor, Frank Sinatra, James Dean, Mia Farrow, Sophia Loren sitting on Elvis's lap—thinks that "real beauty comes from the inside. I used to photograph tons of very pretty girls. There's a difference between a very pretty girl, or a very beautiful girl, and somebody who was truly beautiful. Audrey was to me . . . that was where my feeling of beauty was, and Hollywood necessarily with all the makeup and all the fantasy things, it wasn't my thought of what beauty was."

WOULD AUDREY . . .

Disappear for the weekend? Absolutely. Especially during an arduous shoot when she needed her rest. After she married and bought the place in Switzerland, she disappeared for *years* (no, just kidding . . . actually, she hung out there between movie gigs and fielded offers).

Turn off her phone/cell phone/BlackBerry? No, but she would probably have left them at home and gone for a walk if she wanted a break.

Multitask? No! Audrey was not one of those people who balanced her checkbook while attending the opera (don't laugh, we've seen it), or put on makeup in the car while driving, talking on the phone and slurping coffee.

Instead, Audrey focused on whatever she was doing at the time—having a fitting, writing a speech for UNICEF, goofing around with the dogs—and moved on to the next thing. This gave her focus and equanimity. Plus, she accomplished more.

"When she reads, she reads; when she fits, she fits; when she talks clothes, she talks clothes; when she sits under a drier, she simply sits and dries," reported *Cosmopolitan*. "She is the only actress I've ever had who doesn't gab, read, knit, wriggle, pick her teeth, or eat a lettuce and tomato sandwich," said her hairdresser.

Disguise her voice when answering the phone? No. While Jackie Kennedy pretended to be her maid (at times) when she was home and did not want to be disturbed, Audrey never did this. Her voice was too distinctive, for starters.

Follow a particular religion? No. As she said, "I have enormous faith, but it's not attached to any one religion . . . my mother was one thing, my father another. In Holland they were all Calvinists. That had no importance at all to me." Another time, she noted, "Nature is my religion."

Admit that she learned some positive lessons from her mother? Yes. AH has said that her mother was raised in a "strict, Victorian upbringing," and that she had suffered from her mother's emotional reserve. "She was very demanding of us—of me and my brothers." Still, the baroness taught lessons that stayed with Audrey for life: "'Manners,' as she would say, 'don't forget, are kindnesses. You must always be kind.' . . . She was always very adamant about that."

Ever get angry at someone? And if so, how would she show it? According to Rob, "It depended on who Audrey was mad at—if it was someone she didn't know well, or care about, then she could walk away. But not even disdainfully; she just would absent herself. But if she was mad or hurt by someone that she loved, she was hurt where she couldn't express her hurt. Again, she would absent herself, but in a different way. You could see the hurt in her face. If she was mad at her boys, she wouldn't punish them, but she would, without intending to, show the hurt. And that of course affected them much more than giving them a smack on the behind."

Think of others? Yes. Stu Crowner saw this when he worked with her on the script for *Gardens of the World*. "I have tried to raise my kids with the idea of considering the other person as much as you do yourself. For example, when Audrey answered the phone, she said 'Hel-lo! Hel-lo!' Now, the reaction that would give the caller is, 'Oh, she wants to hear from me!' which is nuts, of course, because she doesn't know who is on the line. But it's part of that generosity of spirit. And she made you feel good, and she was doing that on purpose. . . . Why does everyone say she had this regal stature? I think it has to do with this generosity of spirit."

Take the high road? Yes. Gregory Peck thought "Audrey definitely had a good heart, there was nothing mean or petty. She had a good character—she didn't have any of the backstabbing, grasping, petty, gossipy personalities that you see in this business." Janis Blackschleger, who produced *Gardens of the World*, the last television project that Audrey worked on, felt that "Audrey represents the better version of yourself—you never felt less for being in the room with her, you felt more."

chapter 4

Home Studies

"I am always looking forward to going home,
just being at home with my loved ones and
my dogs, and that's where I love to be!"

–AH to Peter Jennings, ABC News *Person of the Week*

Audrey loved her home. She loved *being* home. Perhaps because her Hollywood life was so public and so demanding (she referred to it as "rather a circus"), and her childhood had been so tumultuous, but Audrey's home life, her private life, was deeply important to her. "I could survive without working," she once said, "but I couldn't survive without my family. That is why my private life has always taken precedence."

In 1965, Audrey bought a beautiful eighteenth-century stone farmhouse in Tolochenaz, Switzerland, called La Paisible, "the place of peace." Surrounded by an extensive orchard, vegetable, and cutting garden with meadows edged in gray fieldstone, here, finally, was a place Audrey could be herself.

Not surprisingly, Audrey's eight-bedroom home was a light, airy place, decorated for her enjoyment, not for a world-famous movie star. It was carefully, perhaps sparely, furnished, and Audrey knew the history of each piece of furniture. Her decorating style was described by Audrey Wilder as "non fattening—just like Audrey."

There were lots of flowers, white wicker furniture, bright paintings, and the occasional Daumier sculpture in the large rooms, nothing heavy. According to Jeffrey Bilhuber—who is one of the top decorators in the world and has worked with Hubert de Givenchy, Mariska Hargitay, Anne Bass, Iman and David Bowie, Peter Jennings, Anna Wintour, and others—"This house is geared to work—the ladder-backed chairs in the dining room, the scrubbed surfaces, the white rattan chairs. But then you see baskets of flowers and clear material, that is an acknowledgment that you can have beauty as an accompaniment to function."

However one describes it, La Paisible was Audrey's home, and she lived there the rest of her life.

While there, her days were spent in the garden, the kitchen, or with friends and family. She did not wear makeup at home, saying, "I hope you don't mind—this is my time." When she was not shooting, she rose about 7:00 a.m. and breakfasted lightly on a poached egg and whole wheat toast with jam. One of her favorite things was to feed buttered toast to her dogs.

Her gardens were her joy, and there was nothing she liked better than to put on a pair of jeans and muck about in the garden. Audrey loved flowers, and there were so many at La Paisible, it seemed that only she and Giovanni Orunescu, the gardener, could keep track of them all—hydrangeas, crocuses, daisies, dahlias, lily of the valley, and lavender to line the walkways.

At La Paisible, Audrey found her center. "Today there are so many people, so many things, so many emotions, and the more there is, the less I want. The more man flies to the moon, the more I want to look at a tree. The more I live in the city, the more I search for a blade of grass."

Jeffrey Bilhuber has his own take on Audrey's private style. "My image of Audrey's home is with her legs tucked under her and a book and no makeup, in a very comfortable chair with a very good light, and I bet that was her favorite place to be—home. It wasn't the red carpet, it probably wasn't the film set! Home was more fun, and she probably felt more safe there."

FAMILY MATTERS

What was the main reason Audrey loved La Paisible, and worked to keep her private life so thoroughly out of the media? Her family.

| Audrey as Daughter |

From all accounts, Audrey's mother was a bit of a tough guy. According to Rob, she was "a superior woman," but "biased and intolerant and critical of most everyone, including Audrey."

Ella van Heemstra was a baroness, and she liked people to know that she was a baroness, which did not go over particularly well in America, and sort of galled her daughter, who was the most down-to-earth person in the world. Rob always felt that Audrey's mother was proud of her daughter, and loved her—she just couldn't express it to her.

And Audrey, sensitive as she was, suffered for it.

Still, Audrey was exceedingly solicitous of her mother, knowing, on some level, that the sacrifices she made getting them both to London after the war had kept the wolves from the door when Audrey was a struggling chorus girl.

Once Audrey had her great success, she took care of her mother.

When *Gigi* opened in New York, she wrote to a friend that she wanted to show her mother the town when she came to visit. Invited to stay at George Cukor's home to attend the 1966 Oscars, she couldn't wait to see him, but added that if her mother could come down to see her from San Francisco (where she lived at the time), then the two of them would go stay at a hotel.[16] For the last ten years of her life, the baroness lived with Audrey at La Paisible.

For whatever reason, Audrey's mother and Mel Ferrer did not get along. Perhaps because they were both two strong-willed individuals, with Audrey in the middle. The baroness loved James Hanson, and considered him a very good match for Audrey, but did not feel that way about Ferrer.[17]

And as we mentioned earlier, Audrey also took the time to repair the situation with her estranged father (privately and away from the press) and very quietly took care of him, too, throughout his life.

| Audrey as Mom |

Audrey loved children—she had always loved children. As she said, "I was born with an enormous love of people, of children. I loved them when I was little! I used to embarrass my mother by trying to pick babies out of prams at the market. The one thing I dreamed of in my life was to have children of my own."

Audrey was, needless to say, practically the Best Mom Ever. She had gone through such struggles to become pregnant, enduring

---

[16] Despite AH's fears that they might be a bother, they both ended up staying at Cukor's.

[17] Like most of Audrey's friends, the baroness was similarly unenthused about AH's marriage to Andrea Dotti, brightening only when Rob appeared on the scene. The fact that he spoke fluent Dutch, no doubt, helped the situation.

several heartbreaking miscarriages. (Years later, when Sean was grown, she confided to him, "That was the closest I came to feeling that I was going to lose my mind.") Like Nancy Reagan and Sophia Loren, she was confined to bed rest for most of her second pregnancy. When her two boys—Sean, in 1960, and Luca, in 1970—were born, she was ecstatic.

As a mom, Audrey cared.

Her thoughtfulness for her friends and those she loved, her studiousness with UNICEF, movie scripts, and public speaking, her attention to detail, was like nothing next to her love for her two boys.

When Sean or Luca had a test at school, she was practically more nervous than they were. When Sean had a role in the Christmas pageant at the little school he attended in Tolochenaz, Audrey helped him with his lines. When she wore a Spanish riding costume for a *Vogue* shoot, she had them rustle one up for Sean, too.

Since she believed that her career had contributed to the demise of her marriage to Mel, she more or less retired during her second marriage, to Andrea Dotti, and moved to Rome to devote herself to her family. In 1988, she recalled, "I had to make a choice at one point in my life, of missing films or missing my children. It was a very easy decision to make because I missed my children so very much. When my elder son started going to school, I could not take him with me anymore, so I stopped accepting pictures."

As a mom, she had few rules. Manners were important, of course. And the boys were limited to a half hour of television a night, and one Coke a week. But other than that, Audrey wanted them to be happy.

| Audrey as Spouse |

While no one really knows what goes on between two people, particularly a husband and wife, we do know that Audrey was an incredibly supportive spouse. Placing her trust as an actress in Mel once they married, and advancing his career—and hers—as much as possible, she was also a traditional wife who created a beautiful home for him.

When she was married to Andrea, she stopped working to devote herself to her husband and children. Living in Rome as a doctor's wife, she often brought Andrea's lunch to his office. She stayed in each of her marriages for far longer than was (perhaps) good for her, for the sake of her children.

If nothing else, she gave each marriage her best shot.

| Audrey as In-Law |

"Low-key" was one way of describing Audrey's place within the familial axis. To the outside world, Hepburn was a star, but when she was home, she checked her ego at the door.

When she was married to Dotti and living in Rome, she invited Dominick Dunne to her in-laws' home for dinner. He recalls a scene where Audrey happily played the low-maintenance daughter-in-law.

"We were invited to dine at Andrea's mother's house. And it's a big Italian family, and the mother was a big Italian lady and had a lot of power about her. I was a total outsider, passing the spaghetti and doing this and doing that. And Audrey was absolutely a part of it—and in that house, Mrs. Dotti was the *queen*. It's not like Audrey was the movie star. Audrey and everyone else there absolutely deferred to her. And I thought, boy, if that's not a lady, I don't know what is—and that's instinct, that's not what you learn in finishing school."

Interestingly, although she totally cut Mel out of her life after their divorce, she remained close with her in-laws. Mel's sister Mary, for example, remained a friend for life.

| Audrey as Godmother |

Can you imagine how fabulous that would be? The closet-raiding possibilities alone leave one speechless. Not to mention what an excellent gift-giver she was.

Doris Brynner, then married to the actor Yul Brynner, lived just minutes from Audrey in Switzerland and was one of her closest friends. Audrey was godmother to her daughter, Victoria. As Victoria recalls, Audrey was not a mere figurehead, but someone who "always gave incredibly sound advice whenever I had problems with my parents or boyfriends or if I was scared about something."

Audrey gave solid professional assistance, too. When Victoria was just beginning her career as a photographer, Audrey invited her to shoot her UNICEF trip to El Salvador in 1989. Although she had been around Audrey all her life, it was the first time Victoria was with her in a professional capacity. Brynner recalls that "it was a great opportunity to watch her deal not only with the suffering people in the field, but with all the UNICEF officials, the governments, the media, constantly bouncing from one to another."

While there, they had a particularly wrenching visit to Quito's most poverty stricken areas, and afterward, the two women visited the beautiful La Compañía church. "We stood there next to each other and held hands and each said her own little prayer," Victoria recalled. "After what we'd just seen, it was very moving."

A few months later, Audrey went to Victoria's home for her birthday. As a gift, she handed her a basket. In the basket was a bird's nest Audrey had found in her garden, and in the bird's nest, a little hand-painted paper bird, and under the bird was a cross set with diamonds and rubies. The card said it was for that moment they had spent in the church in Quito.

Victoria has worn it every day since.

MAKING A HOUSE A HOME

Style has nothing to do with money. It costs next to nothing to put a *cache peau* of flowers on a table, or use pretty napkins at the dinner table. Whether in her clothing choices, her reading choices, or decorating, AH mixed high and low with equal aplomb—she loved hot dogs for lunch at La Paisible, but also had fresh green beans from the garden. You can do the same.

The main thing is that your home (like your wardrobe or accessories) should reflect your life. Your interests. And your history. Audrey's taste level was so secure that you walked into La Paisible and you knew Audrey lived there.

You can do the same for yourself. And don't be afraid to show some personality—collect things from your travels and scatter them on the table for the heck of it. . . . Just make sure they are small trinkets so they don't obscure your guests! At one memorable dinner, Diamond Jim Brady gave sand buckets and shovels to his guests so they could dig for real jewels in a sandbox. We're not saying you need to go that far, but you get the idea.

Audrey loved fresh flowers throughout her house. She had a cutting garden, as well as an allée of sixty rosesbushes that Givenchy had planted to celebrate her sixtieth birthday. (Nice!) So whether you live in a studio apartment or a 15,000-square-foot McMansion, you can easily use some of Audrey's advice and make your home lovely.

| The AH At-Home Checklist |

Music. Audrey liked all kinds of music—from jazz and David Sanborn to Bach—so we know she would have had it brightening the halls at La Paisible. Although the iPhone might have been too much technology for her—heck, it's too much technology for us—knowing how much she loved music, we have the feeling she would have had an iPod.

Scented candles. Audrey used the green Rigaud candle at home in Switzerland, as did Pamela Harriman and the Kennedy women alike. For a time, Diana Vreeland's exceptionally handsome husband, Reed, was the first U.S. representative for this jet-set favorite. A perfect hostess gift, it comes with a small travel size in a very chic zebra-striped tin.

Diptyque candles. Favored by writers Marina Rust, Amy Sedaris, and every chic Parisian we know. We like "Oranger," but choose your favorite: They last forever. There is also Alora Ambiance scented sticks (which might sound strange, but trust us, try these and you will become as addicted as Sarah Jessica Parker and Liv Tyler).

Personally, we love James de Givenchy for Taffin candles. Beautiful. The best. Track him down and try to persuade him to sell you a few—you'll thank us.

Flowers. Move beyond the usual glass florist containers. Small Limoges sugar and creamers make ideal vases. For the table, cut low bunches of the same flower (or any greenery) and put them at either end or the center.

China. Audrey's china was (of course) white. According to Rob, she had rough country crockery for everyday use, and then the good stuff.

While Baccarat and Tiffany & Co., or Limoges, can be the go-to place for crystal and silver, Williams-Sonoma has well-priced silverware and glassware, and you won't burst into tears if you accidentally drop something. Charlotte Moss's shop in NYC is utterly di-vine, as AH would have said—perfect for gifts and housewares you won't see everywhere else.

| Setting the Scene |

Herewith, the importance of setting a good table—which you know Audrey knew how to do. Whether hosting an outdoor luncheon for a children's birthday party or dining à deux with Rob on a snowy winter's night, Audrey didn't just wing it.

And if we need further inducement to sit and eat a proper meal, sociologists now tell us that families that eat dinner together have more successful children, who get better grades, have greater self-confidence, and are less likely to abuse drugs or alcohol—probably because moms don't miss anything! (While Ron and Nancy Reagan were known for dining in front of individual TV tables at the White House, we stubbornly persist in following the example set by Audrey.) Besides, nutritionists believe that mindless eating in front of the set is part of what has been leading to our country's rather astonishing weight gain.

Here is table-decorating advice from Robert Rufino, Vice President of Creative Services/majordomo of Audrey's favorite place in the word (cue the soundtrack) . . . Tiffany's.

✎ **It is always good to have a theme (or point of view),** no matter how big or small the occasion. And it is always nice for guests to come to a table with a surprise—whether it is a dinner party for eight or a quiet dinner for two.

❧ **Giving your guests little gifts** always add fun to the night.

❧ **Begin with lush flowers.** (Of course, little vases of flowers can work for a quiet dinner for two.) Buy roses early so they open. Full blown are better than buds. You do not always have to use flowers; a centerpiece can be created by using some of your favorite objects on the table. Example: Use porcelain objects— dogs, dragons, etc. I have a collection of miniature busts of different shapes and heights, which create drama on a beautiful black and white tablecloth. I also love using clever place cards.

From Robert, here are some themes for the various seasons:

❧ **For spring:** Make a play with blue and white.

❧ **For summer:** Work your table around shells.

❧ **For fall:** Think harvest, using pumpkins, gourds, and autumn leaves for a centerpiece, and use a lush brown velvet tablecloth.

❧ **For the holidays:** Go mad with layers of plaid.

❧ **And lastly, for a New Year's celebration:** Use a theme around Truman Capote's Black and White Ball—i.e., lush white flowers and an assortment of black and white candles of different heights. Give your guests black and white masks to wear and always, always use the best quality napkins, ones that are starched and pressed.

Iron Like a Star

Okay, we're not saying you need to be able to iron your own shirts—well, okay, we are, because Audrey knew her way around an ironing board. When she was shooting *Gardens of the World*, Janis Blackschlager said that AH was one of the most low-maintenance stars she had ever worked with. Shunning the typical Oscar-worthy demands of a cappuccino maker, her own gym, and all the red M&M's picked out of the bowl, she did her own hair and makeup, and only requested a hair dryer and an ironing board and iron in her hotel suite. When Janis arrived at AH's door for the 5:00 a.m. call, she often found Audrey up and at 'em, standing at the ironing board, ironing whatever Ralph Lauren outfit she was planning to use that day.

So here goes.

For starters, it is always better to launder your clothing at home, since over dry-cleaning generally wears out your clothing. Instead, be like the Italians and air out your clothing after a big night rather than sending it out.

Now, about that shirt. Hardcore homebodies suggest hand-washing your shirts in the sink. But since we are not Martha Stewart, er, have a life, we launder the shirts in the washing machine and take them out and briefly hang them up to get some of the moisture out.

While it's still damp, take the shirt, wrap it in plastic (a plastic grocery bag is fine), and stick it in the fridge overnight to get cold. This makes the ironing even more effective.

Taking the shirt and, laying it on the board, use a hot iron and iron it in this order: collar, yoke and shoulder, cuff, then sleeve and body. Start on the left if you are right-handed, and the opposite side if you are left-handed. If you do not have steam, use a spray bottle to mist the shirt. If your shirt is still a bit damp, use the "dry" setting.

Hang the shirt on a hanger and gently press the collar down with your hands. Button the top two buttons to keep the nice, crisp fold.

And just think, hey—if it works for Audrey, I can at least try to iron once in a while. Your shirts will thank you, too.

AH AND LES CHIENS

One cannot discuss La Paisible—or Audrey's personal life—without discussing Audrey's dogs. In addition to being one of the style setters of this (and practically any) century, Audrey was one of the great dog lovers of all time.

"Who thinks you're as fantastic as your dog does?" asked Audrey.

According to AH, practically no one. It was no surprise that when she moved to Hollywood—that cruel intersection of appearance, ego, insecurity, and success—Audrey had a little dog, Famous. Famous was practically as famous as his owner, accompanying her on film sets, while she got her hair done, appearing in many an Avedon fashion shoot, even having a cameo in *Funny Face*.

Like many celebrities (well, except for Audrey), "Famey" was not particularly well behaved: He peed on Audrey Wilder's silk Louis XIV chairs (Audrey was mortified; Audrey Wilder thought it was hilarious). He was wildly jealous of Ip, the baby deer Audrey had to bond with in preparation for shooting *Green Mansions*, and acted out by hiding behind lamps and barking madly.

"You have to understand—Famous *adored* Audrey," explained Bob Willoughby. For a time, perhaps in danger of becoming the

Judy Garland of the celebrity canine set, Famey was even prescribed doggy tranquilizers.

Still, Audrey loved him. She loved all dogs. In later life, after a succession of Yorkies, she would have no less than five Jack Russell terriers, among them Tupper, a gift from Audrey to Rob for his fiftieth birthday, because he had never owned a dog. "My little hamburgers," Audrey called them. They all slept in their mistress's bed—Porthault sheets and all—because, as Audrey joked, she "couldn't find a basket big enough for all five of us."

In fact, Audrey and Rob disliked spending more than two weeks away from home because they did not like to leave their dogs, and Dominick Dunne remembers being in a hotel suite with them as they called Switzerland to check on a particular dog that was ill. With the possible exception of Oprah Winfrey, few celebrities love their dogs so absolutely as Miss Hepburn.

As she put it, "I think an animal, especially a dog, is possibly the purest experience you can have. No person, and few children . . . are as unpremeditated, as understanding, really. They only ask to survive. They want to eat. They are totally dependent on you, and therefore completely vulnerable. And this complete vulnerability is what enables you to open up your heart completely, which you rarely do in a human being."

Invite Audrey into Your Home!

Here is some of Jeffrey Bilhuber's advice on developing some Audrey Home Style.

1. **Know Yourself**. Audrey's home was so successful because it was a representation of who she was—you walked into that house and you knew: It was hers! You can do the same. Whether you live in a farmhouse or a city

penthouse, make sure your home represents who you are, not what someone talked you into buying.

2. **Have a vision.** According to Bilhuber, "refinement is the message. Clarity. And clarity comes from a clear mind, it's just that simple. It has nothing to do with 'I only like red, or I only like blue!' It is knowing your mind, being confident and competent in your decisions."

3. **Clear out the clutter.** "Edit, edit, edit. I can't say this enough. Try to look at your space the way an editor (or a realtor) might. And don't be afraid to clear out the clutter and put it in storage. It will make your space look bigger, too."

4. **Flowers—indoors!—lots!** Audrey loved fresh flowers, and nothing makes a home more inviting than flowers. In the winter, you can have a large bowl of oranges, lemons, or green apples to make a statement.

5. **Beware of getting too matchy-matchy.** Don't buy furniture in whole sets. You want the room to go together, but you don't want it to look prefabricated. Audrey knew her home so well that she could tell you where each and every piece came from—and what you don't want is for every piece to come from the same place. That's like ordering the same thing for dinner for a month—too boring. More than anything, you want your home to reflect your personal taste, which, we are hoping, is not plain vanilla.

   If you are not sure what to do, study design magazines to see a look that you like, or have a close friend whose taste you admire look at the room and give an honest opinion.

6. **Favorite things.** When you travel, buy something—a postcard, a seashell, a souvenir—to remind you of that happy time. Create a small grouping of them on a mantel or side table.

THE ART OF THE PERSONAL LETTER

In studying the finer points of star behavior, it seems clear that the well-timed note is what separates the truly well brought up from the arrivistes. Socialite Babe Paley (like Princess Diana and Jackie O) sat down and wrote her bread and butter notes the night she came home from a dinner party or event.[18] George H. W. Bush was famous for typing notes himself (on a typewriter, not a computer) to practically everyone he met, and this garnered him a heck of a lot of goodwill across the political spectrum.

Thankfully for us, Audrey was a great letter writer, and many of her letters can be found at the AMPAS Library in Beverly Hills. She favored bonded blue stationery with her current address—generally Switzerland or Spain—printed in smaller, darker blue ink in the top left corner. In her finishing school script (an open, almost left-handed slant), she wrote pages upon pages of her thoughts, travel plans, possible future projects, and daily routine to directors William Wyler and Fred Zinnemann. She was democratic in her correspondence and, in later years, wrote to photographer Steven Meisel, hairstylist Garren, makeup artist Kevin Aucoin, designer (and friend) Jeffrey Banks (often including photographs of one of her dogs), and Ellen Mirojnick, the costume designer for *Always*.

The point is that if AH could take the time to write, surely you can, too.

---

[18] She also trimmed the edges of the stamp with a tiny pair of gold scissors. Now you know why Truman Capote said of Mrs. Paley, "She was perfect. . . ."

| The Specifics |

While some believe that modern conveniences like the cell phone, e-mail, and BlackBerry have made snail mail obsolete, we believe the opposite: Today, a personal note has even more impact, and will definitely separate you from the crowd. Ladies, or gentlemen, if you want to impress your possible intended, send a typed love letter on business stationery to the office (making sure to scribble "personal" on the back flap). It is far more effective than sending flowers, and will last forever. Colin Cowie, Oprah's favorite party planner, is a man who has style practically down to a science, and he leaves his personal stationery at the florist, wine shop, and chocolatier so that when he sends a thank-you gift, they include a handwritten note on his stationery.

We're impressed.

As to the specifics, the note does not need to be long, but it should be directed to the person you are writing to, and convey your personality. Remember that you (like Audrey) are memorable, so make your notes as individual as possible, too. And in case you are wondering, AH signed her letters (to friends) "xx" or with a little sketch of a heart, and then her name.

| The Finer Points |

Any piece of paper will do, of course. But the social (and fashion) crowd favors the four-by-six-inch flat card, with your name engraved across the top. If you have oversized, flamboyant handwriting, it should only take a sentence or two to fill up the page, and with your name at the top—even if the recipient can't read your hieroglyphics— they should be able to figure out that you wrote some sort of a note thanking them for some sort of . . . something: perfect!

| Stationery We Like |

Crane's

Smythson

Mrs. John L. Strong (along with the flower budget and
the open bar, save this heavy-duty expense for
when you get married)

Kate's Paperie

Tiffany & Co.

Kate Spade

Or, you can be Very Audrey and just scribble a note from the (no doubt four-star) hotel where you happen to be staying. So few people take the time to write letters these days that anything you say will be considered pearls of wisdom simply because you took the time to write it down.

In L.A., the Chateau Marmont gives guests personalized stationery when they stay with them. A nice touch.

HEALTHY LIVING AT HOME

"The only time to eat diet food is while you're waiting for the steak to cook," said Julia Child, which is something Audrey would probably agree with 1,000 percent. While she ate lots of salads on the set in her glory days, between shoots she loosened up and enjoyed herself. (In 1953, meeting Hedda Hopper for the first time, when HH comments on her "sensational" figure, Audrey shrugs it off, saying, "I've put on a little weight—on my holiday in England. When I'm not working, I put on weight.")

> *"I am not a huge snacker, but I eat awfully well at meals and all the things I like."*–AH

When Audrey was home and out of the public eye, what did she eat?

Audrey ate well. Like many of our European friends, she did not graze or eat between meals, but sat down and ate proper meals (china, silverware) at the table. "I am not a snacker," she said in 1992, "but I eat awfully well at meals, and all the things I like." You would never see Audrey at the food court in a sweat suit with lettering on her backside, munching on a Cinnabon.[19]

For the record (from her cook, her friends, and even photographers like Bob Willoughby and Steven Meisel), Audrey loved to eat. But for the most part—let's be honest here—she ate healthfully, and she's wasn't gorging on Big Macs and supersized soft drinks. "She's disciplined, like all those ballet dames," was how Humphrey Bogart put it.

"I'm one of the lucky ones," she said. "I seem to have a sort of built-in leveler. I've a tremendously good appetite—I eat everything, *everything*—but as soon as I'm satisfied, a little hatch closes and I stop."

Like most women of her occupation, class, and generation, Audrey didn't eat a lot of junk food (for starters, it didn't really exist then—certainly not in the faux, corn syrup and sucrose laden way

---

[19] Besides, she hated Danishes, and for the opening scene of *Breakfast at Tiffany's* she wanted to eat an ice-cream cone instead, but director Blake Edwards refused.

we know today). She loved pasta with marinara sauce or penne alla vodka, and fresh vegetables from the gardens at La Paisible—bright salads, string beans sautéed in olive oil, quiche on a bed of home-grown lettuce, something for dessert. She even loved hot dogs, one of her all-time favorites.

"I don't like fancy food at all," she admitted. "I much prefer an extremely simple meal that's exquisitely done . . . a perfectly cooked steak, a beautiful salad, some raspberries."

According to Florida Broadway, the cook Audrey hired when she was in Los Angeles shooting *My Fair Lady* and then brought to Switzerland to live with her for two years, "For a tiny woman, she had an enormous appetite. She loved to eat, and they had all kinds of things with butter and cream. They liked chocolate soufflé, roast duck, rich things. Once, when Yul Brenner came to dinner, I made this roast duck and oh, you never heard such carrying on over duck in all your life."

And when a cook was not around, Connie Wald said that "Audrey loved nothing better than to be in the kitchen with the children."

Julie Leifermann, who traveled with Audrey for three months shooting *Gardens of the World*, thought Audrey had a wonderful understanding of proteins and carbohydrates, and of eating to give herself energy. Part of this was her experience in young adulthood. As Audrey remembered, "I lived through the war with very bad nutrition and found how tough it is to live without enough meat or vitamins or milk."

With Audrey, there were few empty calories. "She ate a lot of fruit," Leifermann remembers. "She ate fairly simply, because she didn't want to bog herself down with huge meals, because we would be getting up early to shoot in the morning. When she was working or constantly traveling, her instinct was to eat healthy, and eat the things that gave her energy, with occasional indulgences here and there, but it wasn't anything you'd really notice."

Before it was popular or even on the radar of most Americans, Audrey ate organically. At home, she ate good food of very high quality ingredients, and although many of us are starting to catch up with her, in this sense her instinct was more European than American at the time. She was also "green." At La Paisible, she grew corn, lettuce, tomatoes, tons of basil for her favorite pesto, as well as apples, cherries, pears, peaches. She even had walnut trees and hazelnut bushes.

Okay, while it's pretty obvious from just looking at Audrey that she ate well—what about the fun stuff?

Like most of us, Audrey loved chocolate in any form. "Let's face it, a nice creamy chocolate cake has a lot for a lot of people; it does for me." She often had a square or two of dark baking chocolate in the afternoon. (And unlike most of us, she could stop at just one square.) In Audrey's early Hollywood career, costume designer Edith Head was amazed at her ability to eat a hot fudge sundae or four éclairs at one sitting. With her neighbor Doris Brynner, she enjoyed vanilla ice cream with hot fudge on top. Sometimes, when visiting Los Angeles, she, Rob, and Connie used to go to the Hamburger Hamlet on Sunset after catching a movie in Westwood. They always split the Ultimate Hot Fudge Cake for dessert.

| Now, About That Figure ... |

And what—if anything—did she do to maintain her famous gamine figure? As an adult, Audrey was five feet seven inches, 110 pounds. Yes, she ate well. But part of it—probably most of it—was genetics. Audrey was just built the way she was built (she said that she looked exactly like her aunt). Nearly starving during the war also permanently altered her metabolism. In addition, Audrey was always very physically active. While she never had a personal trainer, set foot in a gym, or jogged around Central Park the way your average star would today, she loved to walk, and stretch, and took the occasional dance class when she could.

"Exercise?" Audrey once said (in a comment that, once again, confirms why she is our personal hero). "No, no. That's too much like school. I like to be free. There are too many musts in life without adding exercise.

"I'm totally unsporty," she admitted. "I expect that comes from all those years of dancing and making movies and not having the time. . . . I think of myself as an outdoors person, without being in the least athletic. I love to walk in the country—to be out in the clean air. I walk for miles by the sea. I walk in the sun."

When she was home at La Paisible, after dinner she liked nothing better than to get outside and take the dogs for a walk through the countryside. And this was not just a stroll—Audrey *moved*. Asked by a friend why she walked so fast, she said she thought it was in response to her mother, who walked slowly.

A lot of Audrey's appeal was simply her energy. As Steven Meisel or Jeffrey Banks (or practically anyone who crossed her path) can attest, people just liked being around her. "Her calm quality of purity and integrity is rare," thought Cecil Beaton.

Once, when asked how she managed to stay so youthful-looking (which is really just another form of energy), Audrey commented, "I'm just lucky. Healthy and lucky. It's the way I was born, my physical makeup, my bones or whatever. Let's say that I don't do anything in particular to live healthily, but I try not to live unhealthily. I know when I need sleep and try to get it. If I feel like eating pasta, I do, and I am a great pasta eater. But I don't do only that. Some people go through life eating any old thing and then suddenly they are exhausted and wonder why they are losing their figures."

Like her waistline, her philosophy rarely changed. When asked in January 1992 if she had any personal beauty secrets, Audrey said, "If I had them, I'd make a fortune. But I know what helps—health, lots of sleep, lots of fresh air, and a lot of help from Estée Lauder."

Charlotte Moss on Bringing Audrey (into Your) Home

Charlotte Moss is an interior designer, best-selling author, and product creator who believes that "learning how to really live is a lifelong process." Some advice from a pro . . .

- Like Audrey, I can't remember a time when I was not drawn to beautiful things. I want to be surrounded by them at home and will always be exploring what makes a home beautiful-gracious-delightful.
- One must never feel reluctant to experiment in their own home. Enthusiasm, curiosity, and determination with a dash of fearlessness will usually equate to something original.
- Your home reflects more than you know: Generosity and kindness are the rugs; hospitality the furniture; curiosity the objects; and originality the placement . . . Enthusiasm, joy, and vitality are the fragrance that fills the air.
- Family photos, fresh flowers, happy music, a warm fire, and comfortable chairs conveniently arranged . . . isn't that the simple formula that says "home"?
- Audrey's self-confidence should inspire many. After all, how many girls would admit—as Audrey did—that they'd rather have more closets than a swimming pool?

WOULD AUDREY . . .

Use a decorator? No. Although her cousin in style, Jacqueline Kennedy Onassis, had some of the greatest decorators of the twentieth century passing through 1040 Fifth Avenue (and sometimes tried to avoid paying them by writing a personal check because she knew they would not cash it), Audrey's style was all her own. She used designer patterns to cover the soft furnishings. She mixed first-class artwork (among them, a small Daumier bronze) with wide, white couches, lots of flowers brought indoors, and silver-framed pictures of family and friends lining the tabletops. Not surprisingly, although there were dozens of silver-framed pictures of children, friends, and family, there was only one lone photograph of Audrey—a signed Cecil Beaton portrait of her in *My Fair Lady*, tucked behind all the others.

And she loved the color white. Here's a tip: If you want to bring some Audrey Style into your domain, don't think pink—think white!

Give career advice to her children? Not really, but she did give Sean advice on learning his lines for a school play.

When Sean was about twelve, he was going to be in a school play, acting out *Le Malade imaginaire*, by Molière, a famously diffi-cult—but funny—monologue by a hypochondriac, and Sean was concerned about learning his lines.

Audrey told him, "Just read it. Don't try to learn it." Later, she advised him, "This is what I do—I read my lines right before I turn the lights off at night and then again when I open my eyes in the morning."

"That's it?" he asked.

"That's it."

Let the dogs on the furniture? Come on, you know she would— heck, she let them sleep in the bed with her, designer sheets be damned. In a mild nod to practicality, she had the couches in the den covered in a rough pink nubby pattern to hide some of the wear and tear.

Know how to run a house? Yes. And the gardens outside.

Have help? Yes. Audrey had a cook when she was married to Mel, a housekeeper, a nanny when her boys were small, and a gardener/outside man. Giovanna, her housekeeper, stayed with her for forty years and was truly a part of the family. Audrey took great pride in her home, loved to cook and more often than not prepared the food for her own luncheons and dinner parties herself, was an extensive gardener, and arranged all of the flowers.

Pimp out the kids? No way. Bob Willoughby remembers Audrey as "a great mother, very protective. She never wanted Sean to be photographed for release. She had the fear that a lot of famous people had about kidnappers, particularly in Europe. She brought Sean to the set of *The Children's Hour* and I promised they wouldn't be used in the magazine. . . . I kept them until he was grown."

Take a nap? Yes, when she could. Although it was never possible (obviously) during the big shoots for *My Fair Lady, Breakfast at Tiffany's, Funny Face*, etc., once AH retired, she got up early and got going in the morning, a holdover from her filmmaking days, as Connie Wald remembered. But when she could, she would duck in and take a short nap in the afternoon. She also did this during the shooting of *Gardens of the World*. Since the light is best in the morning and late afternoon (the "magic hours," in filmmaker's terms), Audrey took a break at midday.

Like to swim? Curiously, Audrey loved swimming but had a morbid fear of getting her head wet. She never knew the reason why, really, but Rob thinks it might have been because her two older brothers might have dunked her sometime when she was a girl.

Drive? No. Audrey did not like to drive, leaving it instead to a studio driver (when making a movie), Rob, or her gardener. On July 14, 1958, heading to the studio to begin shooting *Green Mansions*, she was involved in a fender bender at the intersection of Beverly Drive and Santa Monica Boulevard. When the woman she accidentally rear-ended, an aspiring actress by the name of Joan Lora, learned who she was, she sued Audrey, claiming she had suffered neck and back injuries.

Mel, being resourceful, hired detectives to follow the woman, and when the case came to trial two years later, they saw that Ms. Lora was not injured after all, and the case was dismissed.

The whole incident left Audrey so shaken that she rarely drove again.

Shop on the Internet? She probably would have, within reason. Audrey was not a huge techno-junkie. Although she did not live to see the explosive rise of the Internet and the enormous cultural changes it has afforded, she thought cell phones (then in their nascent form — think: Michael Douglas talking on a shoebox-sized phone while walking on the beach in *Wall Street*) were intrusive and did not like portable phones at home in Switzerland.

According to Connie Wald, "Audrey liked to shop, but she didn't *shop* shop the way some women do for entertainment." But once she got the hang of it, we think she might have liked some of the following sites.

bergdorfgoodman.com (their magazine, *BG* is beautiful)

vivre.com

patio.com (Where Jeffrey Bilhuber gets the white wicker furniture à la Audrey that we know you now want)

containerstore.com

ralphlaurenhomecollection.com

Bring her work home? No. As Sean recalls, "We weren't a film buff family. She didn't bring it home. She didn't talk about it. She didn't sit there and show us the movies."

Have a hobby? Not in the traditional sense. Audrey did not golf, play tennis, ski, go sailing, or ride horses. That said, she loved to read, listen to music, have friends over, garden, and sketch (just not at the same time). Once, when asked by an interviewer if she had any hobbies, she replied, "Not really. I don't collect things. I sketch—but not at all well.[20] I should like to have more records than I do. I played the violin at seven years. I haven't had time for hobbies. I really worked. That's the trouble. I led a secluded life."

Love children and dogs? Yes—in the adorable versus vulnerable ratio, babies and puppies were perhaps the only things on the planet that could possibly match Miss H.

Go green? Absolutely. Because of her experiences during the war, Audrey was an early proponent of eating fresh, healthy foods. La Paisible was also practically a self-sustaining farm. And Audrey definitely would have stocked up on eco-friendly lightbulbs at Home Depot or verilux.com.

Live in a big city? No, and alas, this is our loss. As much as we love the image of Audrey as Holly Golightly wafting up the stairs of her New York City brownstone, the effects of the war and her childhood, and perhaps her celebrity, stayed with her. She once admitted that she "hates anything that crowds me" and counted her long walks alone in the country near her secluded Swiss villa among the "joys of life" and went there as often as possible.

---

[20] Take our word for it: Audrey sketched beautifully, and wrote poetry in letters to friends.

chapter 5

On the Road

"I live out of a suitcase."–AH

As a world-famous actress, Audrey spent

a tremendous amount of time traveling all over the world to film sets. This chapter is life on the road . . . whether it be another city, away for the weekend, or hightailing it to Paris for three months. In her glory days, Audrey was not a minimalist. She did not travel light. She did not wear flip-flops or shorts on an airplane or—god forbid—lug a full-sized pillow into the coach section. No, as someone who brought fifty-two suitcases with her when she traveled to her next film set (along with a typed, numbered listing of the contents of every case so she could find Mel's cufflinks in an instant), Audrey believed that you *can* take it with you—and she did.

And for the record, when the studios were paying, Audrey went first class, natch. In later years, she occasionally hitched a ride on Ralph Lauren's or Anne Cox Chambers's private jet. But according to her son Sean, Audrey generally rode coach to save money on her UNICEF trips. So if she could make do in steerage without bitching about it, so can you.

Travel used to be glamorous. Travel used to be fun. Possibly because it was so expensive and so few people actually *got* on a plane (hence the term "jet set"), there was something inherently romantic about airplane travel. One only needs to visit the Louis Vuitton Museum in Paris, or know that Prada started out as a luggage maker in Italy, to know that travel *used* to be exciting.

To cite one example, at the end of a film shoot, Bill Holden, who, granted, had a pretty bad marriage, carried thousands of dollars' worth of traveler's checks (ask your parents: This was pre–credit cards), and he would walk up to the counter and buy a ticket and get on a plane to Africa. Or Paris. Or anywhere. And just split.

Sounds great, doesn't it?

In the old days, you could smoke and drink and enjoy Chateaubriand with impunity on airplanes—heck, it was almost encouraged. Remember the scene in *Two for the Road*, when Audrey almost gets into an argument with her husband, played by Albert Finney, because he won't buy her a pack of cigs to enjoy in first class (and this is on an airplane, not in a nightclub, mind you)? Classic.

When Diana Vreeland traveled, she carried a Vuitton hard-sided makeup case, specially outfitted with a dozen small bottles of Stolichnaya, as well as lemons, limes, and a small knife to cut the citrus with. Now, *that's* traveling.

Nowadays, you can barely carry a lipstick or a pack of gum onboard without getting frisked down by an overzealous security guard. While you used to be able to carry a tall bottle of Evian onboard and look like a real world traveler, today you can't bring any liquids onboard . . . save the $4.00 midget bottle of water you bought in the concourse.

Still, we must do the best that we can, and herewith are some tips to maintain your own state of Audrey Equanimity.

FIRST-CLASS TRAVEL STYLE

Whether traveling private, first class, business, or coach, here is some Audrey-inspired advice to maintain your own personal aura of first-class style.

| Preflight |

Ordering meals. When you book your flight, if they offer a meal (a big *if* these days) and you are in coach or business, order vegetarian or Kosher, even if you are not, as they will have to make your meal fresh and there will be a better chance at eating healthfully if you get fruit or a salad, or whole grains.

Get a manicure/pedicure. Face it, if you are going to have to take your shoes off before you pass through security, you want your feet looking sharp! You *know* Audrey would have. And did.

Airline lounges. If you travel first class, you automatically get access. If you travel a good deal on coach, consider joining the lounges of the various airlines[21] so you have somewhere nice to hang out when

---

[21] For example, American Airlines' Admirals Club.

waiting for your flight, with great reading material, fresh food, and comfy chairs (as opposed to, say, Starbucks, or sitting on the floor in the waiting area), especially considering the endless flight delays we experience today. If you are really stuck on a layover and feeling indulgent, many will let you join for the day for a nominal fee.

Packing Tips

- First of all—and we are sure this sounds rudimentary— make a list of the different events you have, and what you might wear to each. After you have been traveling (and packing) for a while, you can do this mentally, but in the beginning, make a list so that you don't forget a vital item— like the shoes or accessories that go with a certain outfit.

- Depending on how much luggage you want to bring, and where you are going (Nepal? Los Angeles? Is it business? Your honeymoon?), you might want to pare down the list (*very* un-Audrey), or just bring pretty much everything with you.

- If it is just a weekend, or a few days away, you can use a duffel, but for anything close to a week, we like a large, soft-sided suitcase so that you can bring everything you need and still lay your clothes flat. If you are going on a longer trip, or to Europe, you can bring a second duffel to put running shoes, hair dryer (if you need to bring it), odds and ends, etc. But in general, if you get one good-sized suitcase, you should be able to get everything in there.

- Here's an old-school tip: tissue paper! Lots of tissue paper! Some people say that you should pack your clothing in dry-cleaning bags to keep them wrinkle free, but unless you have a very special outfit that you are worried about getting messed up, this seems more bother than it is worth. Just lay everything as flat as possible, with the heavier items—jeans, blazers, suits—at the bottom of the case, and shoes along the sides. We generally don't use tissue (although our grandmother did) unless we are bringing some sort of special couture or evening gown to some gig, say, in London.

- People who travel a good deal have doubles of makeup and toiletries packed and ready to go for when they have to hit the road. If you pack the night before, this gives everything time to settle, and the next morning, you can put even *more* things into your bag.

- Modern fashionistas, and people who travel a lot, swear by the ziplock bag (small and large sizes). Put your lingerie and bathing suits in separate bags, squeeze the air out, and close them, to keep them easy to retrieve.

- For toiletries, separate your larger bottles from non-liquid and put in plastic bags. And one lifesaving tip from our travel-savvy friends: If you are completely type A, or have someone packing for you, transfer your liquids to smaller, reusable containers (you can get them at Boots or Muji). Otherwise, open the lids and squeeze the air out of your toiletries, then close them. They will look sort of squished, but there is something about letting the air out that causes them not to explode in-flight and ruin your clothing. And your life.

- Places like Louis Vuitton and T. Anthony still sell separate shoe carriers. Very good in theory, if you have the space and the inclination. To save on space, you could tuck your socks in your shoes (if you wear them these days; very few fashionistas do).

- Invest in decent luggage.[22] In her heyday, Audrey had a set of Louis Vuitton (that Rob Wolders believes must have been given to her by the company). Jerry Hall keeps her lingerie in an LV hat box and carries that on board. In her later years, Audrey used two large canvas suitcases that Rob had picked up in London.

Be a good tipster. And we don't mean e-mailing *Us Weekly* about a celeb sighting at LAX. Keep a few singles or a five-dollar bill in an outside pocket so you can reach it quickly to tip the check-in guy, etc.

Finally, we generally check our suitcase at the curb so we don't have to lug it around the terminal, and just have our carry-on bag. Although we have friends who swear by Never Checking In And Carrying Your Stuff On Board, we only know men who do this, as they do not have the shoe/lingerie/maquillage issue.

Also, use one of those specially approved locks (you can get them at any good department store), so that security can open your bag and inspect it, in case they have to.

| In Flight |

Dress, for god's sake! If there's a time to ask yourself *WWAD?*, boy, this is it—AH always dressed. We're not saying show up like you're going to a dinner party, but a neat pair of jeans and white shirt and a well-cut blazer or cardigan will go far.

As an editorial observation, we do not understand people who

---

[22] Like Marilyn Monroe, Nancy Reagan, JFK, and Elton John, we are partial to T. Anthony.

get on airplanes as if they are going to the beach—shorts, exposed midriff, practically barefoot—if for no other reason than how do you expect to be taken seriously? And not to get paranoid, but if something happens and you need to evacuate, you want to be covered. Besides, they tend to crank the AC in airports and on planes, so if you don't dress properly, you are going to freeze the entire time.

And although it is unlikely that any student of Audrey's would need this advice, please keep in mind that gym wear belongs *in the gym*. The first time we went to Paris (admittedly, years ago), we were dumbfounded at the hordes of American tourists in matching warm-up suits, T-shirts, and windbreakers, marching in lockstep down the Champs-Élysées. While it might work in your hometown (it might even be a look in your hometown), if for no other reason than national pride, please, leave it home.

If you must wear sneakers, think Keds or trim Euro-style Adidas, not clunky running shoes. Personally, we prefer leather shoes for comfort and style, to say nothing of the fact that airport personnel will take you more seriously and, possibly, bump you up a class.

And finally, ladies (or gentlemen): If for no other reason than travel is inherently romantic, and you might meet someone special, it behooves you to dress properly, and if you need further encouragement, simply ask yourself, What *would* Audrey do? (And act accordingly.)

| In-Flight Necessities |

Bose headphones. Hear that chorus of angels singing? Whether you buy the original or a copy, Bose is a *lifesaver* for any sort of public transportation. We don't mean to be antisocial (well, okay, sometimes we do), but put it on at the first outburst of a howling baby or your too chatty seatmate, and the noise of the outside world disappears. Every road warrior we know owns one.

iPod. If AH had one of these, she probably would have enjoyed listening to her favorite jazz.

Something to read. Audrey read Graham Greene and Jeffrey Archer for relaxation. When traveling abroad, a friend we know buys the latest hardcover biography that has not yet been published overseas, reads it on the flight over, and hands it off to the purser on his way off the plane. Now, that's style.

Or you can always settle for the latest issue of *Vanity Fair*.

Something to eat. A turkey sandwich with mustard and lettuce on whole wheat, some almonds, an apple, or an orange. We have heard that Donna Karan eats nothing in-flight, and brings her own black mug, which she hands to the stewardess to keep filled with hot water and lemon slices. That is admirable, but let's be honest: On a long flight to the coast, we need something to look forward to.

Besides, we sat next to a supermodel recently, and she brought on her own large salad with chicken slices (bought in the airport). She ate that, and then had bits of the first-class meal—the fresh fruit, the ice-cream sundae with chocolate sauce for dessert, and seconds. She then shared her copies of *Us*, *InStyle*, *Time*, and *People* with us, so not only was she beautiful (and about six feet two), she was also Audrey Cool.

Cashmere wrap. Or a small cashmere blanket with fringes, *not* a pashmina. Every model and fashion editor we know carries one on-board. If you are trolling for a Christmas gift or have just won the lottery, Hermès makes one, while Brora in London makes a slightly more affordable version. Audrey always had one throughout the years to keep her cozy on film sets and airplanes. (For the true Audrey-philes who must know, her wrap in later years was navy.)

Porthault pillow. One Best Dressed Lister we know brings a small Porthault pillow onboard to rest her head upon. So chic!

On the other hand, if this is overkill and you need to edit, go for the Bose, the iPod, something to read, and the cashmere wrap.

Notebook. For the Great American Novel you are working on. After years of using everything from the green-marbled school notebook to beauties from Papiro in Florence, we swear by Moleskin. Favored by van Gogh, Matisse, Hemingway, and Sean Penn, as well as every screenwriter, director, and art director we know, they also make great hostess gifts.

Meds. We have no problem flying—we actually enjoy it—and Audrey never had a problem, either; in fact, she used her downtime on airplanes to write love letters. But we have a few friends who don't, and they tend to pop a few Excedrin PMs (or something stronger) so they can sleep through it all.

That being said, germs seem to be the big thing on planes, and some folks swear that if you drink some Airborne before you fly, and again when you land, you won't catch a cold. And while we would not know from experience, the vitamin-laden Airborne is also said (by Oprah Winfrey and others) to help with hangovers.

The fashion tribe swears by Emergen-C, those chic little packets you get in the health food store, while makeup maven Bobbi Brown favors David Kirsch's vitamin/mineral powder. (Please note: This is not to impart any medical advice, and all of these OTC cure-alls must be dissolved in water before drinking. You'll love the cute fizz.)

Oh, and something else we've heard from people who fly a lot who are mildly germ phobic: Whether in first class or back in steerage—whatever you do, *do not order ice in your drink.*

Meditate. Or close your eyes and just breathe. Take advantage of the fact that you are miles away from your everyday life, and no one can find you.

Work on your hobby. Georgia O'Keeffe had never flown on an airplane until she was in her late sixties. She was fascinated by the very act of flying, and so moved by the experience that she pulled out her watercolors and began painting studies of what became her memorable *Above the Clouds* series.

If possible, be like Audrey and try to maintain some of that childlike wonder of the romance of travel. You'll be a better person for it.

Fly private. We used to date a guy who, no kidding, flew his own jet. It was cool, and it's amazing how quickly you get used to it.

In her later years, Audrey and Rob were invited to fly with Ralph Lauren and a group of friends to Lauren's home in Jamaica, on his plane. When they got there, the women were dressed the way they would have been in the 1940s and '50s—with suits, and even hats! Rob laughed at the memory. "In part, because Audrey would be there, out of respect for her, I suppose. And there would be Audrey in jeans and a polo shirt, but she always had a well-cut blazer so that she always looked extremely elegant."

But the great thing about flying private (besides the obvious *luxe, calme et volupté* aspect of the whole thing) is that you can bring anything you want onboard, and no one cares. Several trunks containing your entire winter wardrobe? No problem! A gas grill, fireworks, fifty-pound sacks of rice, a Shetland pony?[23] Sure!

When flying private, all we can say is: Act as if this is no biggie. "Are we leaving from Teterboro/Butler/Montrose?" is an acceptable question. "Wow—is this *yours*?" is not. Most of all, be low-key. Act

---

[23] And for the record, Audrey did none of these things (well, except for the sacks of rice during a UNICEF tour). We are just illustrating a point.

like you've done this before. Pretend you're getting on a crosstown bus (which you are, sort of).

Yes, the ultrasuede lining the walls of the cabin is cool, as is the low vase of Dutch tulips and freesia on the sideboard (a sideboard?), and often there is a steward to get you a fruit tray, the *Wall Street Journal*, or some Perrier. Which, given global warming and all, seems like an extreme waste of, well, pretty much everything. But you can just put your feet up and relax in your leather chair, read *The New York Times* in peace, thinking of Audrey, and ponder your fortunate life.

| L'hotel–Once You've Arrived |

Charm the front desk. In case you are wondering, staffers who remember Audrey staying at the Hotel Plaza Athénée *still* miss her. We're not saying you need to bug the GM, but make friends with the front desk when you check in . . . in case you need something later on.

Watch the Jim Morrison behavior. We have a friend who is a concierge at the Four Seasons (Oscar Central in L.A.), and he asks everyone to remember that hotels have cameras in all of the elevators, hallways, and stairwells. He also told us some amazing backstage gossip about a movie star and her volatile rapper boyfriend who showed up unexpectedly, and the man she eventually married dashing down the back staircase, struggling to get his trousers on before the other guy found him and killed him. But that's all we're saying. . . .

Many people, apparently, check into a hotel and undergo some sort of expense account mania. Whether because of that, or the lack of proximity to home base, they go off the deep end. "They act like they're on another planet," Mr. High End Concierge says wonderingly, "like they've never stayed in a hotel before." Trust us: Management knows exactly (well, pretty much) what you are up to. "The only place we don't have cameras," he wants us all to know, "is in the rooms themselves. That would be illegal."

Audrey, needless to say, never had this sort of behavioral problem. Ever. She walked out of her front door, every day, as if she were walking down a red carpet. Even if it was just in sneaks and a pair of jeans to walk the dog.

Rearrange your room! Nothing says star behavior like rearranging your hotel room the way you like it. Elvis Presley had a prescribed ritual (well, his minions had a prescribed ritual). Check into the biggest suite on the strip, turn on the television set, put his current reading material on the nightstand, crank the AC, and have the blackout drapes drawn (and, if need be, line the windows with tinfoil to block out the light).

Now, Audrey did none of these things, but since she often found herself living in hotel suites for months at a time, she took the time to make things more livable. When she was married to Mel and staying at the Hotel Raphael in Paris, for example (also one of Natalie Portman's favorite places), management knew to take her things out of storage and rearrange the rooms the way she liked them. So the entire suite was transformed to their taste with their own pictures, rugs, table lamps, bed linens, vases, cushions, silverware, crystal, tablecloths, decanters, and even Audrey's favorite white Limoges ashtrays.

Audrey's memory was so exact that one time after she checked in, she called the front desk and wondered about a particular little side table.

"In another suite," she was told.

Would it be possible to return it to her room? And then suggested where it might be placed.

Of course.

❘ A Room of One's Own ❘

When you are on the road, personalize your room with framed pictures of your family or friends (or your pooch!) to remind you of them while you are there.

Clean out the refrigerator and have them cart away the mini bar—too much sugar/alcohol-induced temptation.

Light a scented candle. Have them remove the ashtrays if they bother you.

Bring your own iPod. Most hotels have speakers so that you can listen to your own music.

If you are uncertain about the amenities of a hotel, bring your own bath gel. Kiehl's or Vitabath makes some great stuff.

While the Duke and Duchess of Windsor traveled with their own bed linens and pillows, as did Babe Paley, we're not saying you have to go this far. Besides, part of the fun of staying in a really great hotel is scoping out the bed. (And you might get some ideas about upgrading your own bedroom at home.)

•   •   •

When you arrive at your destination and don't feel like ironing, try this traveler's trick: Hang your clothing in the bathroom and crank the shower on high to get the room all hot and steamy (obviously be careful to hang your outfit so it does not get wet). Close the door and leave the shower running for about five minutes. Go in and turn the water off, quickly get out and shut the door, and let your clothing hang there for about half an hour. You might not have to iron at all.

| Something Very Cool to Keep in Mind |

Audrey was essentially a private person, and somewhat shy, and perhaps frightened, at times, by all that was expected of her, and yet she got out there (meaning, the world) and acted, and tried, and created something that lives beyond her, even today, a generation after her death. So we will say this: If you have the chance to travel, to contribute, to improve someone's life in whatever small (or large) way, to go off to see the world, to ride a Vespa in Rome, or enjoy an ice-cream cone in the Tuileries one bright afternoon . . .

Go—Audrey would encourage us today.

Through the creative actions of her life, and the courage she had to move beyond her privileged upbringing, Audrey shared herself with the world and lived a big, gracious life, enjoying lifelong friendships with Gregory Peck, Cary Grant, Hubert de Givenchy, Fred Astaire, James Garner, Sean Connery, Ralph Lauren, Jeffrey Banks, and hundreds of people whose names we may never know—but who met her once, and never forgot it.

WOULD AUDREY . . .

Fire the posse? Yes. Audrey was a fairly solitary person. She had her husbands, and the boys, of course. And she was close to her mother her entire life, and Hubert de Givenchy, and a few close girlfriends, and later, Rob. But Audrey was not a wreckin' crew kind of gal. Perhaps because her life was so public, she admitted to enjoying being alone sometimes.

Be practical? Yes. Audrey was surprisingly practical. A friend remembered her as being able to fix leaky faucets, to replace fuses and even fix tape recorders that had malfunctioned. If she was planning a trip, she bought her tickets well in advance, and it was not surprising that she kept such ordered lists of her travel necessities.

Talk to the person in the seat next to her? Yes. Well, actually, the person in the seat next to her would probably speak to her first.

Brown-bag it? Yes. And not only for herself—for friends, too. In 1989, Leendert de Jong, programmer of the Dutch film festival "Film and Fashion" (which had honored Audrey), and a friend visited her. After spending a few days with her and Rob, it was time for them to leave, and Audrey asked them what they would like for lunch to take with them. De Jong and his friend protested, they didn't need anything, but Audrey insisted—what did they want on their bread? One wanted cheese and butter on his sandwich, the other plain cheese.

On their way out the door, Audrey handed them two small Chanel shopping bags as they kissed her and said good-bye. Halfway to Venice, they stopped and opened their bags. Inside was a picnic lunch with real glasses and two slips of paper—one with de Jong's name on it, and one with his friend's.

With butter, and without.

chapter 6

"A Very Stylish Girl . . ."

"How do I look?" AH as Holly Golightly,

Breakfast at Tiffany's

Audrey was known for her style and her beauty, and that certain je ne sais quoi that made her a movie star. In this chapter, we really get into it, a how-to primer on what made Audrey the icon she still is today: fashion, makeup, accessories, her closet and yours.

Audrey wore jeans, exercised (a bit, but nowhere near Jane Fonda's mania), always looked amazing, and had very definite opinions about what she would and wouldn't wear. And now, so can you.

Here, we explore how to get the look, including: the importance of the brow; how to make up for your lack of a twenty-inch waist; education and cultural interests as aphrodisiac; the exceedingly effective smoking and exercise weight-loss program. It's all here: style lessons from the most stylish woman in the world—and what would surprise us to know about her.

AUDREY'S TAKE ON AUDREY

And what did Audrey think of her looks? Believe it or not, she was self-conscious about her upper arms (she thought they were too thin) and her feet (too large). In an extremely revealing 1953 interview with Hedda Hopper, she admits, "I've always wanted really feminine shoulders that sort of slope down." "Come on," said Hedda Hopper (rightly so), "you have terrific shoulders."

"I swear to you that's true. Ask my mother. She's heard it enough. I've always wanted sloping shoulders."

"You mean like the southern belles?"

"That's right—crinoline and all."

Which proves, we suppose, that even the most beautiful women in the world have the capacity to obsess over the most nonexistent things.

"I don't think I'm at all beautiful," Audrey continued, a luminous twenty-four years old, with *Roman Holiday* weeks away from being released, "and I'm not fishing. I mean it."

We have a really difficult time believing this. But Rob Wolders (and he would know, we suppose) said that Audrey "was almost like a child in that she refused to believe how good she looked. She was extraordinarily modest . . . and it wasn't a kind of false modesty."

THE A(H) LIST

"All style is personal–that's what distinguishes it from fashion." –Fran Lebowitz

---

You want Audrey-esque? We've got Audrey-esque. Finally, the soup-to-nuts (or gamine haircut to ballet flats) primer on All Things Audrey. We're not promising you'll find your own Gregory Peck, but follow these tips and you just might make it to the Best Dressed Hall of Fame.

Make the most of your assets, underplay your flaws. In *Love in the Afternoon*, Audrey mock-complains to Gary Cooper, "I'm too thin and my ears stick out, my teeth are crooked and my neck's much too long." "Maybe so," Cooper replies, "but I love the way it all hangs together." So study yourself and make the most of your assets.

For example, while Audrey was self-conscious about her size-ten feet, she had no problem cinching her twenty-two-inch waist. Everyone's got something wonderful to emphasize — highlight it and ignore the rest.

Have a POV. Whether a movie director, a style icon, or just disagreeing with everything Ann Coulter says on television, it helps to have a strong point of view. In terms of fashion, find what works for you and stick with it. Even as a struggling chorus girl in London in 1945, Audrey (who could do more with a plain white shirt than anyone) knew what worked for her and what didn't.

Encourage your mania. Do you love clothes? Fine, don't apologize. In a world with far too many Casual Fridays (and for the men, this translates into the dreaded chino, golf shirt, and Top-Sider combo), look at it this way: You are injecting some verve (to quote Diana Vreeland) into the world. "Clothes are positively a passion with me," said Audrey, who we know traveled with no fewer than a dozen suitcases in her glory days. "I love clothes so much where it is practically a vice." And also: "Some people dream of having a big swimming pool—with me, it's closets."

And don't think people won't notice if you make the effort. As early as 1954, Cecil Beaton noted in *Vogue*, Audrey "is immaculately shod, whether in pumps, sandals or court shoes."

Her style was subtle, not obvious. "She was the first to make something that's not sexy, sexy," says Cynthia Rowley. With apologies to all the Pamela Andersons and Paris Hiltons of the world, and an entire subset of UGG-loving, lingerie-revealing (or non-lingerie-revealing) Hollywood actresses, don't be afraid to tone it down a little.

Disregard trends. Audrey was unique in her style choices in that she knew what was going on in fashion, but did not follow trends. Instead, she decided, early on, what worked for her and moved within those parameters. That said, she never got stuck in a look: Ballet flats gave way to Ferragamo and Roger Vivier, which gave way to Keds and probably would have led to Manolo Blahnik, had he been designing when she was alive.

And although there was always a very distinctive Audrey look, she never got stuck in one decade. She knew when to put away the perfect Givenchy suits of the 1960s and rock out the pea coat, trim jeans, and biker boots of the 1970s.

Good grooming. Oh Lord, don't get style.com editor Candy Pratts Price—who has befriended, worked with, and socialized with some of the most famous trendsetters in the world—started on grooming and style . . . but she is right, you know.

"It's maintenance—grooming is key. Grooming is *key*! Today you can get a manicure and a pedicure—Audrey was groomed! And you know who looks the same way today—Christy Turlington—you *know* that Christy Turlington takes care of her eyebrows. People don't think that matters, but it does! And when you look at Audrey, it was very significant."

"To be natural is a very difficult pose to keep up."

–Oscar Wilde

Audrey-esque Makeup Tips

Audrey was known for her distinctive makeup that high lighted her memorable eyes. What many people don't know is that she worked with the same makeup and hair team (whom she met on *Roman Holiday*) her entire life: the married couple Alberto and Grazia De Rossi. What they also might not know is that Alberto was so exacting that after applying mascara, he used a safety pin to separate each of her eyelashes to get it right. (A somewhat daunting style tip that Julia Roberts recently used in a movie scene to great effect.)

"A girl can't read without her lipstick."

–AH as Holly Golightly, in *Breakfast at Tiffany's*

We are about to make your life a little easier. Thanks to Darac, the former Director of Artistic Development of Estée Lauder, who now has his own makeup line (and has worked with Cher, Princess Diana, Claudia Schiffer, Evelyn Lauder, and a host of others), he is going to show us how to get some AH magic for ourselves, makeup-wise.

In Darac's opinion, "Audrey's makeup got better and better and better. It's not like she had one look and kept it for forty years. Some women get the aqua blue eye shadow going in seventh grade and just stick with it! She also did something very smart—she focused her features. She never tried to make herself something that she wasn't, she worked with the natural beauty that God gave her . . . which is something we can all learn from today."

Eyes

You have a choice: You can play up your eyes or your lips, never both. You have to make a choice.

Start with mascara and put on one coat.

Then put on an eye shadow color that comes closest to your natural skin color, all the way from the lid to the brow to get a nice, even plane. If you start with a color that is too dark, it's too hard to blend, and you can't go anywhere with it. It's very heavy, and it makes your eye look small. So start with that color all over and blend it.

Take your eyeliner pencil and line the top and the bottom of your lid down by the lash. Add your second eye shadow color that is a darker color, but still a little translucent so you can see through it. Put that on the lid area up to the crease. Blend the top at the crease, where you blink, with a Q-tip, to soften the line, so it's very natural-looking.

Put on another coat of mascara.

If you want to get a little more exotic for evening, follow with a liquid liner just on top, and that will give you a foolproof eye—it's easy, and anyone can do it.

Brows

You also have to pay attention to your brows—they really highlight your face. It's important to keep them clean, and not too unkempt. With Audrey, they became her signature. When she started, her brows were quite heavy, and then as the years went by, they lightened them up a bit so she didn't get "stuck" in one look. I think it's worth having them professionally done so you know what looks good on you, and can follow the line at home.

Lips

Keep your lipstick close to the actual color of your lips. Apply the lipstick as you normally would with a brush. Follow with a slightly clear lip gloss, and then use lip liner only on the edge of the top of the lips, for a soft, natural look.

Powder

Use the least amount of powder, and use a light one with the smallest amount of titanium in it. You don't want to use a heavy powder, as that will instantly age you ten years. Use a brush, and tap off the excess.

Posture   Now, we're not saying you have to walk like a cadet at West Point, but there is a reason AH could wear the simplest nothing and make it look amazing. Chin up, shoulders back, and when you walk into that room, walk in there like you own it—think of AH gliding across that tennis court in that amazing Givenchy gown in *Sabrina* (even if you're wearing chinos).

Lower your voice.   We don't even know if this is possible, but if you can, try to lower your voice; think: dulcet. Think Audrey on the fire escape in *Breakfast at Tiffany's*, singing "Moon River" to herself. No chirpy little Valley-Girl-Paris Hilton-Don't-Take-Me-Too-Seriously speak.

The ubiquitous ballet flat.   Fact: Audrey was the first person to wear ballet slippers in public. The lesson here is, take something from your life (Audrey's first dream was to become a ballet dancer, a wish that was curtailed by WWII and her height) and bring it out into the public. Then, with any luck, it will become a fashion perennial three generations later.

Never enderestimate the power of a good white shirt.   Or trim black trousers, or a turtleneck, or the right haircut that shows off your profile . . . which leads to the second corollary that style has little to do with money. Audrey wore jeans and a polo shirt as authoritatively as a mink shrug or Givenchy ball gown.

Care and Feeding of the White Shirt

Nothing says Audrey like a good white shirt. From the time she first set foot in Hollywood until her final days, Audrey knew the inherent style power of a crisp white button-down shirt.

Models, actresses, and anchormen know that a white shirt is the best option when you are being photographed because the white reflects up and illuminates your face (which is also why saints in medieval paintings are always painted with a halo around their faces). Coco Chanel knew this, and favored white silk shirts with wide, rounded collars under her famous suit, as does Diane Sawyer. And, by the way, that is also why working actresses and models stay out of the sun.

Some Specifics

Go for a straight cut. Not too tight, or fitted. Make sure it fits at the shoulders.

Choose a strong, classic man-style collar and no pockets (which ruin the line, adding bulk and weight). To make it more individual, look for piqué, fine cotton, tuxedo front, tiny ruffles at the bib, or French cuffs (just not all together).

We think untucked is starting to look old. If you tuck your shirt in, check that it is smooth, without wrinkles and bumps, which is why it helps to wear a slim skirt or pants of heavier material (flannel, tweed), or jeans.

Audrey's waist was so diminutive that she could leave her shirt untied and unbuttoned, wrap the ends around her waist, and tie them at the back. Hey—give it a shot, why not?

Iron it. We know, boring but necessary. Think of how fabulous it will look, and besides, do you ever recall seeing a photograph of Audrey in a wrinkled shirt?

Launder it and lightly starch it at home. Dry-cleaning causes yellowing.

The Boyfriend Option. Nothing is more adorable—or says "I have lots of beaux and/or handsome brothers!"—than wearing an oversized man's shirt. A little Annie Hall, a little Katharine Hepburn. When she first came out to Hollywood, AH did a mildly racy (for the time), shoot for *Life* magazine in which she spoke on the telephone wearing only an oversized white shirt. Knowing AH, we are sure it just appeared that way—but the baroness was *not* happy.

The white shirt should be a staple for anyone's wardrobe, and, fortunately for us, there are many options from the most expensive to the Gap. Here are some we like.

Banana Republic. The fashion insider's go-to place for 100 per-cent T-shirts and the white shirt.

Thomas Pink. Your sister found out about this place years ago when she was living in London with her Brit boyfriend (now hus-band), and used to carry them home across the Atlantic for extra-special gifts.

The Gap. Reliable, reliable, reliable, and yes, still reliable.

Petit Bateau. PB is the true fashion editor's favorite. Pricey but amazing. They'll last forever, and whether a newborn or ninety, you will look great in them, too. Don't let the French sizing throw you off.

Anne Fontaine. When you are ready to grow up a bit and move beyond Gap or Banana Republic simplicity, this French woman makes the most stunning shirts (only white—which we love), that are detailed with lace, jacquard, and embroidery. www.anne fontaine.com

Valentino. You can't go wrong with Mr. Val. Our favorite Italian designer always does a few beautiful white shirts each season that are as chic with white jeans as with a taffeta evening skirt. If your ship has come in—or even if you are expecting it soon—pick up a few.

Chanel. Years ago, we spent the afternoon with Audrey Wilder (director Billy's wife), reminiscing about Audrey H, Marilyn Monroe, Nancy Reagan, and Hollywood in the old days. She was a delightful woman and raconteur. In Wilder's memory-filled apartment in Los Angeles, she spoke freely, smoked unabashedly, and offered us the chicest doughnut peaches as a snack. Oh, and she wore trousers and the most beautiful silk Chanel shirt with a long pearl necklace.

Although it is rare to individually tailor a shirt (although, god knows, Wallis Simpson had three fittings for her nightgowns during her early courtship with the Duke of Windsor, and look where it got her), make sure it fits when you buy it. Cotton or silk is best, although sometimes you can get it with a bit of stretch.

Make friends with your tailor. If you've read this far, chances are you already know it, but even if you buy something straight off the rack (especially if you buy something off the rack), get to a tailor and make sure everything fits perfectly. Edith Head recalled that Audrey's Paramount fittings "were of the ten hour, not ten minute kind." As Cameron Silver, who runs Decade, *the* shop in L.A. for all of those vintage Oscar gowns, says, "Your tailor is more important than your shrink!"

The well-thought-out accessory. For all of her almost Oriental restraint, Audrey understood the impact of the properly chosen accoutrement: a small dog, oversized black sunglasses, some borrowed Schlumberger, Cary Grant.

All That Glitters . . .

Audrey bought, wore, owned, and borrowed jewelry from the Big Four—Tiffany's, Cartier, Harry Winston, and Van Cleef & Arpels. Oh, and Bulgari, who did her engagement ring for her marriage to her second husband, Andrea Dotti. During her first success as an actress, she got a diamanté collar for her dog, Famous, from Van Cleef—now, that's (puppy) love. When shooting *Breakfast at Tiffany's*, she wore Schlumberger, and for *How to Steal a Million*, the jewelry was by Cartier.

But mostly (and why are we not surprised?), AH was about simplicity in the bling department. Since she never had her ears pierced, she favored a pair of single-pearl and diamond clips in the 1950s and early '60s.

And in spite of the Cartier and VC&A at her disposal, Audrey was not above the occasional faux piece that Givenchy designed to go with her evening gowns when she attended awards ceremonies in the 1970s and '80s.

Audrey never wore a watch. For some reason, she just did not like them. And yet, she was always on time. When she was married, she wore a simple wedding band, and in her later years, she wore two rings on her left pinkie—one that Rob had given her as a Christmas gift, with some tiny diamonds, and another that was made up of some sapphires Sean had gotten in Hong Kong during his first job.

If Audrey were alive today, we just know she would be wildly addicted—like the rest of us—to the *beyond* exquisite designs of James de Givenchy for Taffin, the handsome and talented nephew of you-know-who.

Ignore age. Audrey said that she sometimes felt as if she were twelve years old; other times, thirty-eight. It didn't matter, she thought, few people feel their actual age, anyway. "I wouldn't be able to tell you who I am because it has never bothered me. I never asked who I am. I don't care."

Don't cancel that *Times* subscription just yet. Let's face it: Whatever *it* was, Audrey had it. Fashion illustrator Joe Eula recalled, "You look into those eyes and suddenly you find yourself agreeing with everything she says." At the core of Audrey's appeal was her intelligence and her personality: a combination of innocence and playful sophistication. "She spoke many languages fluently—English, Dutch, French, Italian, Spanish, and probably others of which I am not aware," said director Stanley Donen. So go to college, read a book (no, *Us Weekly* does not count), watch Charlie Rose. Be informed, be curious, be engaged in life—that is the difference between a pretty face and a truly beautiful woman.

For Audrey, her choice of clothing was not simply about fashion or style (although it certainly was about that), or even projecting her personality out to the world (although it did that, too). Instead, in her increasingly public life, the right clothing gave Audrey a certain reassurance. "Clothes, as they say, make the man," she noted. "But they certainly have, with me, given me the confidence I often needed."

And Audrey never lost her love for clothes. As Rob recalls, "Even in the last months of her life, dressing was important to her. It was like a little girl dressing up. She was herself, you know, she didn't become someone else. But she never lost the fun of dressing up."

We hope you don't, either.

"A fourteen-year-old might not really know Audrey's history as an actress, but she can really love her look, and a fifty-year-old woman can feel the exact same way—which shows you that simplicity and quality wins out."

–Michael Kors

THE PERFECT MAN . . . STYLEWISE

While Audrey had her share of romances, there was one man who contributed the most to her style: Hubert de Givenchy.

It was the summer of 1953, and Audrey was in preproduction for *Sabrina* and had gone to Paris at the behest of director Billy Wilder. She was playing a chauffeur's daughter who grew up on a Long Island estate. Bookish and ignored by the two sons of the house, she goes to cooking school in Paris and arrives at the Glen Cove train station wearing a gray wool suit cut to within an inch of her life. Accessorized by dark red lipstick, white gloves, and a cloche, a gray poodle and a pile of hard-sided luggage, she is the Audrey we know.

Now the definition of chic, she is picked up by David Larrabee (William Holden), who is instantly smitten.

"Don't I know you?" he asks, wondering if her father is in transportation.

Something like that—she says, smiling, mysterious.

It is one of the great film entrances of all time—Audrey in a "jazzy" French suit[24] with just enough mystery to make you wonder. Obviously, some great clothing was needed to make the transformation believable, and no one thought Edith Head, Paramount's lead costume designer, was up to the task. "The kind of glamorous suit we needed for Audrey when she comes back, imbued with the taste of Paris—Edith had no idea what it was," said Billy Wilder.

Unfortunately, Edith did not really "get" Audrey in terms of fashion. In one 1953 Paramount *Sabrina* memo, she "advised Hepburn to stay away from dead black." Which is hilarious, in a way, because Audrey used this color to great effect her entire life. "When you think of Audrey Hepburn—Audrey Hepburn *is* black!" pronounced fashion icon Polly Mellon. "Nobody wore black better than Audrey— she owned it!"

No matter. One of the great friendships—and style collaborations of all time—was set in motion when Gladys De Segonzac, wife of the Paris head of Paramount, called and asked Hubert if he would meet with "Miss Hepburn." Givenchy was intrigued. Just four years older that Audrey, he had opened his own studio the year before on the Rue Alfred de Vigny.

Of course, he assumed she meant Katharine Hepburn, as *Roman Holiday* hadn't been released yet, so there was no reason for him to know this "skinny little nobody" (as Audrey referred to herself).

He agreed.

Audrey showed up at his atelier, all charm and nervous energy. She was beautiful, that he could see. But Hubert was surrounded by the most beautiful women in the world every day. She was both open and shy. She loved fashion and she needed him, or so she said. She was also a little bit goofy. But upon meeting her, he had no idea, really, who she was.

Once the miscommunication was resolved and he understood what she was after, he explained that it would be impossible for him

---

[24] The one everyone's mom, or grandmother, instantly went out and bought.

to help her—much as she said she loved his work—as he was in the midst of preparing his collection and had no time to assist her.

Please, she begged. Please. There must be something.

Hubert looked at her and relented. (How could he not?) And allowed Audrey to try on some of the samples from the previous season's spring/summer collection.

And what a collection it was. Audrey ultimately chose three pieces, and from those three pieces, an entire style—that we are still influenced by today—was born.

In the end (which was really the beginning), Audrey chose something we call the "Glen Cove Suit," the classic French suit she wore at the Glen Cove train station, breaking a thousand hearts; a white ball gown, number 808 of the collection, known as the "Inez de Castro"; and finally, "the Date Dress," the classic little black dress she wore on her date with Linus Larrabee (Humphrey Bogart). A dress to change your life.

Audrey took those three outfits and walked straight into fashion history.

Edith might not have been a designer, but there was one thing she understood: studio politics. A fierce in-fighter (no small thing in Hollywood), she had it written into her contract that she would receive top billing for any Paramount film. So when Audrey invited Givenchy to California to attend the screening of *Sabrina*, she was stung to see that Givenchy was not even mentioned in the credits.

Givenchy, for his part, was too polite to comment, saying that it must have been an "oversight."

In spite of Edith's maneuvering, Givenchy's lack of public recognition didn't matter, because after *Sabrina*, suddenly everyone wanted to have Audrey Style. "Everyone on the street was copying Audrey's hair," said Dreda Mele, the director of Givenchy's atelier, "the way she moved, the way she spoke. Everyone wanted to look like Audrey Hepburn. They copied her for ten solid years after." Writing in *Vogue*, Cecil Beaton agreed: "Thousands of imitations have appeared. The woods are full of emaciated young ladies with rat-nibbled hair and moon-pale faces."

And did Audrey notice her effect on fashion?

"Well," exclaims Audrey Wilder, "when she saw an imitation of herself walking down the street—sure she did!"

With the dawning of *Sabrina*, Audrey and Hubert formed a symbiotic relationship of the most perfect sort. In the wake of her success, Audrey came to believe that she needed Hubert's clothing. "I had a very slim kind of technique," she said. Whether this was true or not was almost beside the point. The fact is, she believed it.

"What helped me out a great deal with the part are the clothes," Audrey said. "It was often an enormous help to know that you looked the part, and the rest wasn't so tough anymore." She later said, most touchingly, that Hubert's clothes made her feel "protected."

For his part, Givenchy was not draping yet another mannequin. In regard to Hepburn, he said, "Audrey knows everything that is good for her. She gives me direction. She is definite."

Audrey and Hubert; with fashion being the least of it, what a partnership.

In the wake of their initial success, Givenchy and Audrey continued the longest-running, most successful fashion collaboration of all time—better than most marriages, most business arrangements, the relationship between most directors and their stars. After *Sabrina*, Givenchy continued with an all-star lineup, designing her wardrobe for *Funny Face* (1957), *Love in the Afternoon* (1957), *Breakfast at Tiffany's* (1961), *Charade* (1963), *Paris When It Sizzles* (1964), and *How to Steal a Million* (1966), as well as the dress for her second wedding, and her sons' christenings. Their thirty-year friendship and their fashionable string of hits was unrivaled, especially today when stars and celebrities depend on a designer or, god forbid, a stylist to tell them what to wear. Audrey knew what she wanted, and she knew who to work with to give it to her.

"I have always considered Audrey my sister," Hubert said. And on some level, he may have been the man Audrey trusted most—certainly before she met Robert Wolders. In honor of her sixtieth birthday, he had an allee of sixty pink rosebushes planted at La Paisible. She even asked him to be her *légataire testamentaire*, an executor of her estate.

He and Audrey understood each other. With their increasingly public lives, they knew how important, how rare, this understanding was. "The two of them were very alike—so rigorous, well organized, concentrated on their work—and behaving so well at every moment of life," observed Dreda Mele. For his part, Givenchy said, "Audrey knows everything that is good for her. She gives me direction. She is definite. You must have people around you who understand the same music."

And unlike her husbands or some friends, Hubert never betrayed or disappointed Audrey. In many ways, he was perfect.

The Original LBD

"When the little black dress is right, there is nothing else to wear in its place." –The Duchess of Windsor

The little black dress. Invented by Chanel in 1926, it was dubbed "the Ford Dress" by *Vogue* because, like the Model T, it became an instant craze, was wildly popular, and came in one color, black. Givenchy brought it to its highest levels of restraint and sophistication in the 1960s, while one person—Audrey Hepburn—became the living, breathing personification of everything the LBD stood for.

The evening dress Audrey wore in the opening scene at *Breakfast at Tiffany's*, nibbling a Danish and gazing at the windows that poignant morning, is probably the most iconographic. But there is also the LBD she wore on her date with Humphrey Bogart in *Sabrina*—encouraging women everywhere to bare their collarbones and submit to the occasional set of pushups (which, god knows, Audrey never did). Or the grown-up and glammed-out version she wore in *Paris When It Sizzles*.

Prior to her death in January 1993, Audrey gave Givenchy more than twenty-five dresses he had made for her, which he keeps in his Paris apartment. One by one he is distributing them to museums around the world. In December 2006, he auctioned the *Breakfast at Tiffany's* dress to benefit the City of Joy Aid, a charity that helps India's poor. At the time it was announced, no one knew how high the bidding might go, since this was, after all, the most famous dress belonging to the most fashionable woman in the world.

But auction insiders knew it was going to be a very serious number. Because one was bidding against not only every designer, every *Vogue* editor, every Audrey fan in the world, but also every Wall Street guy who wanted to impress his wife, Tiffany & Co., as well as three quarters of the population of Japan, China, and San Francisco. If only for bragging rights, there were a lot of Audrey fans in the world who would love to get their hands on the dress—and help charity at the same time.

In 1986, Christy Turlington wore a dress from *Breakfast at Tiffany's* on a shoot for *Vanity Fair*. She was not modeling the dress that was auctioned but the one Holly Golightly wore to visit her beau, Sally Tomato (a mobster), at Sing Sing. As Christy recalls, "We reenacted some of the scenes, with kind of a modern twist—we did a picture with a cigarette holder and coffee in front of Tower Records. A little scene with a cat, that kind of thing."

But beyond fashion, why does Christy think Audrey is such an influence, even today?

"There's something quite childlike and vulnerable about her. I think that kind of playfulness. She just seemed to carry herself with such dignity and grace, and you would never know about the hardships that she endured.

"I guess that's what I respect most, because in our day and age, when everyone knows everything about everyone! I mean, I don't know if she was involved in any scandals, maybe she was. I think she kept a sort of grace that people respected. And I always find that nice, that reserve, that's very intriguing."

The beauty of the black dress, which most women realize, is that it is almost economical. If cost is a concern, copies abound in all different price points—*that* is the beauty of the perfect black dress. As Candy Pratts Price observes, "It can be the same black dress for thirty years—if it's the *right* black dress. You can dress it up and wear it to the Oscars, or your sixteen-year-old niece can wear it with flip-flops and a little sweater. Bare your arms, bare your legs, too, if you are feeling *seduisantes*. Most definitely wear heels."

And finally, for some style advice—who has taken Givenchy's mantle in the LBD department?

While John Galliano (any year, any style) is master of the Most Likely To Be Donated To The Met Costume Institute When You Are Done With It Award, as well as the inevitable "Wow—that dress costs as much as a car!" comment, in considering a dress you can actually purchase, hang in your closet, and wear to dinner, our vote goes to Valentino.

And, by the way, the *original* original LBD that Audrey wore in *Breakfast at Tiffany's* sold for $920,000—more than six times the presale estimate—at auction on December 7, 2006. According to the Christie's Web site, it was bought via telephone by a private European buyer, and set a world record price for a dress made for a movie.

"There are tears in my eyes," said Dominic Lapierre, who sold the dress on behalf of the charity. "I am absolutely dumbfounded to believe that a piece of cloth which belonged to such a magical actress will now enable me to buy bricks and cement to put the most destitute children in the world into schools."

"I can't understand how a woman can leave the house without fixing herself up a little, if only out of politeness. You never know, maybe that's the day she has a date with destiny, and it's best to be as pretty as possible for destiny." –Coco Chanel

THE AH DIET/EXERCISE REGIME

How did AH maintain her enviable (*beyond* enviable) figure her entire life? And, for the record, we have seen her fitting form at Western Costume in L.A., showing her measurements in her late fifties, having had two children . . . and *gamine* does not begin to describe her shape.

Although *miraculous* might.

Like most fashionable women of the time (Babe, Jackie, Gloria Guinness, Diana Vreeland, Pauline de Rothschild, Slim Keith), Audrey engaged in the cigarette/salad as entrée/minimal exercise diet. And what can we learn from her today?

1. The first thing to be aware of is that Audrey had a heck of a metabolism. Part of this, of course, is pure genetics (something you cannot do a thing about). And part of it, unfortunately, is the deprivation she suffered during WWII, when there were extreme food shortages, from the ages of eleven through sixteen (the time of greatest growth for girls). By the time the Allied army liberated Arnhem, AH was down to ninety pounds and suffering from a variety of diseases—asthma, jaundice, anemia, and severe edema, a swelling of the joints and limbs, where the blood literally turns to water.

Her experience during the war explains why AH had such trouble gaining weight, had beer with her meals during film shoots to keep her weight up, and, in fact, could eat bowls of pasta her entire adult life (with great relish, we might add).

2. Trained as a ballet dancer, AH had a great deal of discipline. ("I don't care what anyone says—you can tell a ballerina when she's coming down the street whether she's eighty or twenty!" observes Candy Pratts Price.)

Audrey had an unerring visual eye and just *knew* what worked for her, and what didn't. Living in London after the war, she was discovered by the writer Colette and won the role of *Gigi* on Broadway. Coming over from England on the *Queen Mary* for rehearsals, she ate everything in sight and quickly gained twenty pounds. Upon seeing her, the producers were dismayed to find that their leading ingénue was a bit less sprightly. Adopting an Atkins-esque diet of steak tartare and green salad at Dinty Moore's, the famous Broadway hang-out, Audrey soon returned to her preferred 110 pounds. And stayed there her entire life.

3. AH rarely exercised. Although she took dance classes when she could spare the time in her twenties (and certainly during the filming of *Funny Face*), there is no known evidence of her ever setting foot in a gym, getting on a treadmill, working out with a trainer, sweating to the oldies with Richard Simmons, etc.

Although she was naturally graceful, and moved beautifully, Audrey was not trained in any particular sport (unlike Jacqueline Kennedy or Katharine Hepburn, who were exercise fanatics). When she and Mel lived in Switzerland, she didn't even ski, as the studio insurance policy wouldn't allow it.

But what Audrey did do—which is something we can all do, no matter what our age, where we live, or even our current physical condition—is walk. Audrey was a fresh-air fanatic and walked miles and miles fast—after dinner when she was in Switzerland. So pull out those sneakers and hit the road.

4. Audrey smoked two, and sometimes three, packs of cigarettes a day her entire adult life, from the age of about fifteen on (as did Jacqueline Kennedy and Babe Paley, for that matter). In the old days (i.e., pre 1970 Surgeon General's warning), people were far less vigilant about the dangers of tobacco.

And even today, if you go to L.A. right now, you will see dozens of people (most of whom probably just came from the gym or yoga class) hanging out in the sunshine, enjoying a latte, puffing on a cigarette.

Audrey's profession did not exactly help matters, either. Every model we know smokes. Most actors, too—the Olsen twins, Kate Moss, Kate Hudson, Sean Penn, Charlize Theron, Cameron Diaz, Keira

Knightley, Johnny Depp, Colin Farrell, Winona Ryder, Kirsten Dunst, Brad Pitt, Demi Moore, Catherine Zeta-Jones, Alec Baldwin.[25]

The problem, of course, is that cigarettes will kill you or, at the very least, make you very sick. You might be able to get away with it—like so much else—when you are young, but in the long run, you are better off quitting or, better yet, not starting. If you need a role model, Christy Turlington (rare among models for her college degree and equable poise) gave it up years ago, and even appeared in a public service announcement encouraging young people to do the same.

5. Some people (okay, mostly women) tend to do one of two things when they get stressed—eat more, or eat less. Personally, we have friends in each camp. When Audrey got stressed, she did not head for the freezer and pull out a half gallon of Breyers; she got focused, probably worried too much, and ate less than she normally might. While shooting *The Unforgiven* with John Huston in Mexico in 1958, Audrey learned to her great delight that she was pregnant. Unfortunately, she was thrown from a horse during filming and suffered four fractured vertebrae and a badly sprained foot. Terrified that she might lose the baby, she finished the film in April and, together with Mel, went home to Switzerland to await the birth of their child.

An even greater sorrow awaited her when she went into labor, for the baby was stillborn. The loss pitched Audrey into such a deep depression that Mel feared for her sanity. She smoked over three packs of cigarettes a day, bit her nails to the quick, and lost almost fifteen pounds. At thirty, her grief and heartache caused her to look years older.

It was not until the birth of her son Sean in 1960 that she regained her equilibrium.

---

[25] We are not letting our own subset off the hook here, either. Many, many writers (F. Scott Fitzgerald, Ernest Hemingway, Edna St. Vincent Millay, Hunter S. Thompson) smoked, too.

Quitters Are Winners . . .

Nicotine is supposed to be as hard to kick as heroin. There is the prescription patch, and Drew Barrymore and Matt Damon quit smoking by hypnosis. This is not meant to be medical advice, of course, but here are a few more tips from *The Juicing Bible,* by Pat Crocker and Susan Eagles.

- Maintain constant blood sugar by eating six meals a day, consisting of fresh fruits and vegetables, and a little protein and whole grains.
- Ease withdrawal symptoms with a mainly vegetarian diet.
- Exercise regularly. Walking and breathing exercises are excellent.
- Snack on sunflower seeds and pumpkin seeds. The zinc content may reduce cravings by blocking taste enzymes.
- Eat plenty of oats. Studies show that oats diminish nicotine cravings.
- Soothe the nerves by drinking calming herbal teas, such as chamomile, mint, or ginger. (Christy Turlington found that she had to give up caffeine while quitting smoking, because she associated coffee with cigs.)

| Buff Basics |

This was Audrey's general regime, but for the rest of us mere mortals who do not have her blessed metabolism, how can we get (and stay) in fighting shape?

David Kirsch, author of *The Ultimate New York Diet,* who operates the Madison Square Club and trains luminaries such as Ellen

Barkin, Karolina Kurkova, and actress Kerry Washington, does not believe in dieting. "America is the processed carb capital of the world. You want to eat real food, you need to have a balanced diet, and diets per se don't work. The moment we think diet, we think deprivation, and we don't want to live that way—life is too difficult."

Instead, he advises that we stay away (as much as possible) from processed food and if you would like to jump-start your progress, avoid alcohol, bread, overly processed carbohydrates like white bread, white sugar, high-fructose corn syrup, and high-fat dairy for two weeks.

In terms of exercise, Kirsch believes that movement—of almost any kind—is key. "Everyone can move their body. It's not sets and repetitions and 100 pounds, it's *moving*. You also need to know your body. If walking is easy for you, then maybe you should be swimming, or maybe you should be riding the bicycle, or use the rowing machine. But don't run if you're really overweight, or have bad knees. One needs to pick the exercise that you like the most."

On the West Coast, Gregory Joujon-Roche, founder of the West Hollywood lifestyle center Holistic Fitness, will spend weeks to months getting stars like Tobey Maguire and Brad Pitt ready for movies such as *Spider-Man 3* and *Troy*. Joujon-Roche, who is generally paid by studio production companies for his work, gets script access so he can help his clients with everything from stunt choreography to learning how to gracefully swing a sword.

But when it comes to giving clients exercises that work the whole body, Joujon-Roche says basic moves can have a big impact. If you really want to change your body, Joujon-Roche says men should do fifty push-ups a day, rain or shine. Women should shoot for thirty.

And if you need further motivation, Michelle Pfeiffer avoids wheat, dairy, and sugar (although she admits to having the occasional Krispy Kreme), and runs four to six miles a day. And uses sunblock religiously. And look at how well it works for her.

AH VS. JKO

"Audrey had far more personal style than Jackie. . . .

Jackie took her cues from Audrey."–Vera Wang

In a debate that still roils fashion-conscious *consignetti*, one wonders: What came first, the Audrey or the Jackie? Or, put another way—did Audrey influence Jackie's look or vice versa?

Audrey and Jackie were, along with Grace Kelly, born in 1929. Audrey and Jackie were known for their beauty, personal style, constant search for privacy, and courage. They were also both modern, single (albeit famous) working mothers for much of their lives. However, we believe that in strictly historical terms, Miss Hepburn would be the clear winner in any Jackie versus Audrey throwdown.

Let's look at the time line. In 1951, Jackie won *Vogue's* Prix de Paris writing contest, beating out thousands of college seniors across the country. During the same year, Audrey appeared in tiny parts in films in England and in the stage play *Gigi* on Broadway.

Living at home with her mother and stepfather, Hugh D. Auchincloss, in McLean, Virginia, in 1952, Jackie worked as an "Inquiring Camera Girl" for the *Washington Times-Herald*, asking whimsical questions of men like Senator John F. Kennedy and Vice President Richard Nixon for $56.75 a week.

Audrey appeared in American *Vogue* no less than four times in 1954.

She also shot *Roman Holiday* with Gregory Peck that year, her first "real" role in a Hollywood motion picture, and won a Tony for *Ondine*, as well as a Golden Globe and an Oscar (her first time out of the gate) for *Roman Holiday* in 1954.

Although Jackie followed fashion with the avidity of a baseball fan watching the World Series, Audrey had been close friends with Givenchy since 1952. Jackie, on the other hand, would not be able to afford anything but copies of French couture until she married her husband and he was elected to the White House in 1961. There, averting a possible PR scandal, his father, Ambassador Joseph P. Kennedy, took care of the bills. For political expediency, Jackie's love (and growing collection) of Givenchy originals were kept out of the press, and Hollywood costumer/playboy/Kennedy pal Oleg Cassini was conjured up as her official designer.

"It is not reality, but the appearance of things that count!" the ambassador often lectured his sons and daughters, and in reality, Jackie wore a lot of Givenchy and Chanel smuggled into the country by a variety of ruses, including her sister Lee Radziwill, diplomatic couriers, and stores that catered to the upper class, such as Chez Ninon and Bergdorf Goodman in New York City. At the time, it was even said by *Women's Wear Daily* (then an obscure industry rag) that Givenchy offered behind-the-scene advice for what Jackie should wear to various high-profile events.

Were circumstances different, Audrey herself might have become the First Lady of Camelot. But although the senator was one of the most eligible bachelors in the country, they both knew that as an actress, a European, and a non-Catholic, Audrey did not stand a chance of becoming Mrs. Kennedy. No doubt, this added a certain bittersweet undertone to their friendship. Kennedy was said to be fascinated with Audrey, telling *Time* magazine that *Roman Holiday* was his favorite picture of the year. "She out-Jackied Jackie," said one friend of Audrey's who knew them both.

Instead, Mr. and Mrs. Auchincloss announced their daughter's engagement to the senator, and Audrey went off to the North Shore of Long Island—interestingly, both Jack's and Jackie's teenage stomping grounds—to film *Sabrina*.

In later years, as Jackie's star ascended, the president called Audrey from time to time to tell her how much he enjoyed her latest movie. She even sang "Happy Birthday" to him in 1963, the year after Marilyn's memorable performance, at the last birthday of his life.

Style, talent, heartbreak, and extreme discretion linked Audrey and Jackie, as well as the irony of two innately private, somewhat shy women having to lead such public lives.

Although Audrey was, if possible, even trimmer than Jackie, and Jackie far more athletic than Audrey, their personal styles were not dissimilar. They both favored jeans and sportswear for the day and were capable of seriously glamming it up at night. They shared an intense dislike of publicity for publicity's sake, and adored—and were fiercely protective of—their children. They both smoked, loved chocolate ice cream, wore oversized dark sunglasses, and, because of discipline, a searching intelligence, or merely fortunate genes, aged very, very well.

In the late 1980s, Miss Hepburn and Mrs. Onassis met by chance at the Carlyle Hotel in New York City. The erstwhile princess and the former First Lady, seated at a velvet banquette—what did they discuss, we wonder?

How we would love to have been there.

"Beauty comes from the inside. . . ."-AH

The Audrey Essentials

So you've read this far and you're thinking to yourself, it's *impossible* to be like Audrey—you're an American, your mother is not a Dutch baroness, God did not grace you with such admirable cheekbones (or clavicle), you have so little time, plus, you love baked goods.

We get it. We're with you. But don't let any of this discourage you. Herewith, the pared-down checklist for developing your own Audrey Style.

1. Wear mascara.
2. Stand up straight.
3. Get your clothes tailored.
4. Lower your voice.
5. When in doubt, love.
6. Be generous.
7. Don't kiss and tell.
8. Forgive.
9. Turn around and check the back of your reflection in the mirror before you leave the house.
10. Smile.

And finally, having written all this, we want to leave you with one thought: The way you look on the outside has little to do with true beauty. Don't focus on the externals to the exclusion of who you are on the inside. As Audrey said herself, "Whenever I hear or read I'm beautiful, I simply don't understand it. I didn't make my career on beauty." Some of the most compelling men and women of our time (Mother Teresa, Georgia O'Keeffe, Abraham Lincoln, Picasso) never set foot in a beauty parlor, or a gym, their entire lives. And yet they were extraordinary-looking. So again, in the same way that size, or money, has little to do with style, your purely physical exterior has little to do with beauty.

If Audrey were reading this, she would probably be a bit embarrassed at all of this emphasis on her beauty. So after you have put on your mascara, or gotten your haircut—teach a child to read, call up a friend who is going through some hard times and offer a word of encouragement. Get online and give what you can to UNICEF. We can't tell you how strongly we feel about this—and know that Audrey would, too.

WOULD AUDREY . . .

Buy knockoffs? No. She had too much respect for the work designers did. With the first money she made as an actress in *Gigi*, she bought a Givenchy coat. A faithful customer for the rest of her life, she bought a few things each season.

But Audrey was not a label snob. While she wore Givenchy or Valentino with aplomb, she also wore jeans during her off hours. Or a polo shirt and Keds sneakers.

Like any good jet-setter, she picked things up in Europe and at little shops in Italy (mixing a Givenchy mink "sweatshirt" and trim black trousers with a brightly colored straw Mexican tote in her own distinctive style), when traveling abroad was a luxury few Americans experienced.

Mix high and low? Yes. Jeffrey Banks tells the story of Audrey and Rob being in NYC for UNICEF work. Audrey had left her lipstick at the hotel, so they ducked into a drugstore and bought a $3.99 lipstick. Needless to say, the girl behind the counter was stunned.

Hit the mall? Yes, Audrey loved malls. When visiting Rob's family in Rochester in the 1970s, Audrey used to entertain herself by visiting the Irondequoit Mall and buying gifts for friend's children at the Gap (which was not in Europe at the time).

Look at labels? Yes, and then ignore them.

Use clothing to both reveal and conceal herself? Absolutely. Audrey used fashion to show that she was both whimsical and proper and had a heck of a waistline.

Share her beauty secrets? Sure, why not? She believed in massage—three times a week. She also knew she felt, and looked, better when she got enough sleep, and she liked taking hot baths to relax. She ate a variety of foods, not the same old thing ("and not pasta three times a day"), and took vitamin C or a multivitamin in the winter if she needed it. "I eat healthy food, not health food . . . fresh fruits and vegetables and meats."

But other than that, she "didn't believe in any rigid rules. You have to be as relaxed as possible about food and fitness and the rest of it, or you'll be a slave to your beauty habits. . . ."

Be fastidious about taking her makeup off? Yes. Having worked in the theater, she saw "what not removing makeup really well can do to the skin." She was "a Laszlo girl," but had no "exceptional things that I do or don't put on my face at night. . . . I do believe that good health is the key to good skin. If your skin isn't good, it's a signal that something is wrong."

Lose the earrings? Yes. According to Connie Wald (herself named to *Vanity Fair*'s International Best Dressed List), Audrey's "taste was heavenly, she looked as good in T-shirt and jeans. But her style was just born in her, everything about her was *en pointe*—it was Just Right.

She always used to joke when we tried on earrings, 'Take it off! Less is better—take it off!' "

Although that is sartorial advice, the same applies to close friends, diamonds, and dessert: Less is more.

Have a regular manicure and pedicure? Yes. Audrey had beautiful hands, and favored clear, natural-looking nail polish—never color. When money was tight, she would have done it herself or her mother could have given her one. While struggling to make ends meet in London after WWII, the baroness worked as a manicurist.

Try on a dress properly? Yes. According to Rob, "Audrey was so smart, whenever she would try on a dress, she knew that you couldn't just do it without the hair being coiffed, the right shoes, the stockings, and maybe some earrings to go with it." When she tried on a dress for a big event, he recalled, "She would go into her room for half an hour, and she came back, and I was absolutely dazzled! The cloth suddenly had contour, and shape, and life, and she was so gorgeous."

Leave the house without wearing mascara? Never. Audrey was known for her beautiful eyes, and when she left the house—no matter where she went—she was recognized. Always. We like the pink and green classic Maybelline Great Lash, or Prescriptives.

Be herself? Absolutely. Cynthia Rowley agrees. "There are some things you'll do for fashion, and then at some point, you'll just say— this is not practical! I can't walk in these shoes, or I can't breathe in this dress! Or I don't have this body. Each person has to identify with their fashion role model. For me, it's Audrey. It's just herself. She wasn't going to have surgery—this is how I am, and it was her personality that made her sexy and attractive.

"She's the coolest."

chapter 7

Heartbreak and Solace

"You can't be wise and in love
at the same time." –Bob Dylan

To the casual observer, Audrey's life

looked like a fairy tale—winning both an Oscar and a
Tony Award her first time out; above-the-title billing
with Gregory Peck; lifelong friendships with Hubert
de Givenchy, Cary Grant, Audrey and Billy Wilder,
Ralph Lauren, Harry Belafonte; staying a perfect size 2
without giving up carbs.

Everything she did looked so effortless.

Once, asked to describe her life, she said, "lucky." But seen through the hard lens of history, the cards did not always fall in Audrey's favor. There were her experiences during WWII and surviving the Nazis (she did not like to talk about it, saying, once, "It was worse than anything you can imagine."); her fraught relationship with her mother; miscarriages and difficulty bearing children; the unfaithfulness of her husbands, being dumped by Ben Gazzara in the 1970s (excuse us: Ben *Gazzara*?); the directorial mishmosh that was *Paris When It Sizzles*.

Audrey's life has been fun. It has been exciting and glamorous, celebrated and romantic. But now, we are going to see how Audrey coped when the tide turned against her.

AH LIFE LESSON NO. 1:

| Things Will Not Always Go Your Way |

Audrey's first real professional dream in life was to be a ballerina. Living in Holland during WWII, her opportunities to study were limited and then nonexistent as life grew harsher and harsher, and they struggled to merely survive.

After the war, she and her mother made their way to London, with a scholarship for Audrey to study with the legendary teacher Marie Rambert. In spite of her hard work with Rambert, Audrey was a good five years behind the other young women who had been able to continue their training. In a rare show of resentment, she said, "My technique didn't compare with that of the girls who had had five years of Sadler's Wells teaching, paid for by their families, and who had always had good food and bomb shelters. . . ."

Her height was also an issue. Finally, Rambert brought the issue to a close when she said that Audrey would be a good ballerina—perhaps good enough to joins the corps, or possibly to teach, but she would never be a great ballerina.

As Audrey's son Scan recalled, "My mother told me that she walked home that afternoon, and her dream had died."

AH LIFE LESSON NO. 2:

| Still, Give It Your All |

Part of the reason Audrey had so few regrets in her life was because she always did everything to the best of her ability—which was considerable.

Let's look at her experience during *Green Mansions*, a romantic eco–fairy tale (if such a thing can be imagined) starring Audrey as Rima, a forest sprite, and Anthony Perkins as a compelling romantic lead, directed by her husband, Mel.

As a director, Mel put forth tremendous effort, but he was no Billy Wilder. (Or William Wyler, Stanley Donen, or Steven Spielberg.) In spite of his best attempts, the shoot was a mess. Audrey was exceedingly loyal, never pulling rank as the more successful of the two—how awful that would be for a husband's ego. Instead, she acted like the pro that she was.

As Bob Willoughby, who was on set, observed, "[*Green Mansions*] was Mel's first big directing job, and he didn't have a clue about a lot of it. He would make suggestions and some people on the set would just roll their eyes. Audrey, by that point, had been directed by some of the great directors of the twentieth century . . . but she didn't say a word. She didn't make one comment. She did what she was told and, like any great actor, gave him what he wanted. But I thought that showed a good deal about her character—I mean, Liz Taylor would have screamed at him and told him to go to hell.

"She would do the scene exactly the way he had directed it. So there is that loyalty, and that giving, in Audrey and I quite admired her for that."

The crew members, on the other hand, did not feel the same marital loyalty toward Ferrer, and were so unhappy with his direction that they even threatened to walk off the set.

Green Mansions was Audrey's *Waterworld.*

For once—perhaps for the only time—it seemed as if Audrey had put her instincts aside and simply decided to make a film with her husband. Honestly, it seems as if *Mansions* was sort of a Mel gig, and Audrey went along for the ride. It was the only one of her films that lost money. Sort of a highbrow eco-romance, could anyone honestly believe Anthony Perkins (much as we love him) as a compelling masculine lead? Plus, where was the couture! The Givenchy! Bill Holden! Witty repartee—some sidewalks and a street!

Maybe we're being unfair here. After all, it sounded good on paper—*Audrey as Rima the Bird Girl?*

But then again, maybe not.

• • •

But let's not be too harsh on *Green Mansions*. After all, consider this: Audrey made twenty-six movies in her career, among them the *über* classics *Roman Holiday, Sabrina, Funny Face, Breakfast at Tiffany's, Charade, Paris When It Sizzles, My Fair Lady, How to Steal a Million,* and (our personal favorite) *Two for the Road.* If she had done nothing but *Breakfast at Tiffany's,* that alone would have ensured her entry to the pantheon of cinematic greatness. So surely she is allowed one mild clunker.

And if nothing else, you have to admit that Ip the deer, which followed her around in the movie and lived with her at home, was pretty cute.

Besides, on one level (okay, not the box office level), *Green Mansions* is really about the creative attempt—showing up every day, hitting your marks, and giving it your best shot. On Audrey's part, on Mel's. Even Bob Willoughby's. And in spite of everything, Audrey gives a credible performance and looks lovely in her forest sprite wear. *Green Mansions* had to have had the lowest costume budget of any of her films (having spent the entire time barefoot in one very non-Givenchy dress).

But at least the players were not without humor on the *Green Mansions* experience. Years later, in 1991, at the Lincoln Center Film Society celebration for Audrey, the director Wendy Keys was unable to get (and did not want) a clip of *Green Mansions* included in the proceedings.

"Do you mind," she asked Perkins, who had turned down *Some Like It Hot* to work with Hepburn.

"No, I'm thrilled," he said.

• • •

With the brutal calculation of Hollywood, Mel never directed again. But for his part, he is gracious about the entire endeavor. As a creative player who continued to act and produce successfully, he knew that you roll the dice, and sometimes these things work, and sometimes they don't.

To biographer Barry Paris, he observed, "Directing Audrey was a delight. It was more a matter of trying to present Audrey at her grave and touching best than directing her. She knew what she felt. Revealing it was my job. Perhaps I did not do it well. But Rima remains alive for me, and the film was a creative effort we were all glad we tried."

And for Audrey, her experience on *Green Mansions* was an

important lesson in the price of loyalty, and following (or not following) her instincts.

AH LIFE LESSON NO. 3:

| Keep Going, Keep Going |

In the ensuing years, there was a second and third act to Audrey's life. Shortly after her divorce from Mel, she married Dr. Andrea Dotti, an Italian psychiatrist, on January 18, 1969. Wearing a pink jersey ensemble by Givenchy, with an engagement ring from Bulgari, Audrey said, "I felt twelve years old or maybe twenty, I don't know. I remember only feeling happy, deliciously happy, and Andrea holding my hand."

Their son, Luca, was born on February 8, 1970. And again, she was overjoyed to be a mother.

After ten years of marriage, this union, too, fell apart due largely to Dotti's rampant infidelity. "Italian men are not known for being faithful," he once shrugged, overlooking the fact that he was married to one of the most memorable women in the world. Audrey was further embarrassed that while she was in Switzerland, resting and awaiting the birth of their son, Dotti was photographed leaving nightclubs with a succession of beautiful women. For all of her onscreen serenity, AH was furious that he had chosen to humiliate her.

As she later reflected, "I hung on to both marriages for as long as I could, for the children's sake. You always hope that if you love somebody enough, everything will be all right—but it isn't always true."

AH LIFE LESSON NO. 4:

| If You're Not Happy, Split |

Audrey had great respect for the institution of marriage. But after a certain point, even Audrey had her limits and decided to leave. With each of her husbands, she put up with a hell of a lot, and then, it was as if something inside of her just stopped—for example, when she learned that Dotti had been conducting romantic trysts in their home. "This is not what I signed up for," she said.

"I think she knew from the beginning who [Dotti] was," said Sean, "yet I think she dreamed and hoped that somehow she could change that. And I think she was gravely disappointed when she realized she couldn't." By the spring of 1978, her life with Andrea was effectively over, although the divorce decree would not be final until 1981. As Audrey later admitted with hindsight, "Dotti was not much of an improvement on Ferrer."

AH LIFE LESSON NO. 5:

| And at Least Once, You Will Ask Yourself, "*What* Was I Thinking?" |

Okay, we all make mistakes, and get involved with The Wrong Person, even Audrey Hepburn. Around the time that her second marriage was irrevocably on the rocks, but slightly before she met (sigh) Rob Wolders, Audrey had a brief, inexplicable run-in with fellow actor Ben Gazzara.

It was simple enough, really. They had met on the set of *Bloodline*, a murder mystery that probably sounded better on paper than in real life. Based on the Sidney Sheldon best-seller, it was directed by Terence Young and starred an international cast of (among others) AH, James Mason, Romy Schneider, Omar Sharif, and even Michelle Phillips, who proved—with this gig—that even the famous have school fees, phone bills, and mortgages to pay.

To our eyes, Gazzara could be seen as another—perhaps lesser—version of Mel. A seemingly charmless tough guy who left most of Audrey's friends wondering, "What does she *see* in that guy?" Unhappy, depressed, and adrift when it became clear that her second marriage was not going to work, either, in spite of all of her efforts, Audrey was at loose ends.

They began something of an on-set romance. Perhaps it meant a bit more to Audrey than it should have. Clearly, it meant nothing to Gazzara. He stopped returning her phone calls; once, he even hung up on her. In the end, he made it clear that he was not interested. In a small way (*bastard!*), he broke our girl's heart. If only for a little while.

And we still harbor a secret grudge against BG (real name: Biagio Anthony Gazzara) for treating Audrey so shabbily.

AH LIFE LESSON NO. 6:

| There Is Light at the End of the Tunnel |

It was during her separation that she met and formed an enduring friendship—finally!—with Robert Wolders, an actor and businessman who was the widower of Merle Oberon. Both close friends of Connie Wald's, they met at a dinner at her home in Los Angeles.

It was a sad time in each of their lives. Merle Oberon had died just a few months earlier, and Audrey's marriage was effectively over, so in the beginning, there was no thought of romance. As Audrey told interviewer Glenn Plaskin, "I was charmed with him that night, but he didn't register that much. He was getting over the death of Merle, [and] it was the worst period of my life, one of the low ebbs. We both cried into our beers."

In the beginning, it was quiet between the two of them. Given her marital history, Audrey was extremely hesitant to get involved with anyone, let alone a man seven years her junior. But several months later, Rob happened to be in New York on business when Audrey was shooting *They All Laughed* with Peter Bogdanovich.[26] On his last night in town, he was supposed to go to another dinner party, but met her for drinks at The Pierre. Their conversation was so engrossing that drinks went on for over an hour, and Audrey ordered a giant plate of pasta. And when their time together was closing in on two hours, Rob knew he would be rudely late for his dinner, so he had to leave, and then get on an airplane back to L.A. early the next morning. But after that, they spoke on the telephone practically every day.

Interestingly, Rob had spent the terrible war years near the tiny village of Zwolle, just ten miles from Arnhem, where Audrey had

---

[26] And that bonehead Ben Gazzara.

lived. Although they never met during the war (and Rob was, after all, just a toddler), he and Audrey later shared this experience.

As he said, "Most people associate the war with darkness and deprivation. But they tend to forget that, nevertheless, life goes on. Under those circumstances, which Audrey and I discussed, one discovers things that are quite exciting about oneself, in terms of loyalty to other people, the ability to have fun with very little, your appreciation of life is honed, so any little thing is an encouragement, that life is really all right."

Their friendship deepened, and Audrey—who had been hurt so terribly by her other two husbands—realized that she could trust Rob. They formed a devoted partnership and remained together for the rest of her life.

Some Audrey Real-Life Tips for Trying Times

Talk to your friends or someone you trust. When things got tough, AH herself admitted, "I always had a chum I could talk to," like BFFs Connie Wald and Doris Brynner.

Meditate. Or just sit quietly, close your eyes, and breathe for ten minutes.

Have faith. We are not even sure if we are speaking, specifically, of religious faith here. But just—the sense that there is goodness in the world (along with some great cruelty, too, we know).

Get a pet. "If you want a friend in this town, get a dog," said President Truman. While Audrey was not a big cat person (except for *Breakfast at Tiffany's*), she loved her dogs.

Remain close to your family (unless, of course, they are the source of your annoyances). "Mother and I are not alike, but we get on awfully well," Audrey once admitted in a somewhat veiled comment. "She's a lovely woman."

Take a bath. Audrey was a big believer in the power of the warm bath as a way to relax and recharge.

Cry. Okay, we understand this is a totally chick response, but studies have shown that women are emotionally in better shape than men because they can express their emotions. Sometimes you just have to get things off your chest. Besides, think of how beautifully heartbroken Audrey (as Princess Ann) looked when she had to say good-bye to Gregory Peck in one of the closing scenes of *Roman Holiday*. Well, wouldn't you cry, too?

Get a massage. As a former dancer, Audrey was a big believer in massage. "It's the best thing in the world for you, but you have to choose the right masseur. Bad massage can break down muscle and ruin you for life, but a good one gives you a lot of muscle tone and it can make your circulation go incredibly fast."

AH LIFE LESSON NO. 7:

| The Past Is Past |

As Rob and Audrey formed their life together at La Paisible, he noticed that Audrey never indulged herself in living in the past. "I *loathe* nostalgia!" said Diana Vreeland, and Audrey could have said the same for herself. She knew when to leave the party. Audrey made just twenty-seven films, and although some thought she might have ended her career prematurely, she had no interest in living in the past. In 1988, at a Dutch retrospective honoring her and showing *Funny Face*, she told the organizer, "I hope you found a good print and the colors are still bright." When was the last time she saw it? At the premiere in 1957.

According to Rob, "Audrey was not nostalgic. Cary Grant and Gregory Peck became like family, but not necessarily family that you saw on a regular basis. She would see them, in recent years she saw them at functions, industry oriented events, she saw them more and it was like seeing favorite family members. It was very healthy, not concerned very much with the past."

AUDREY'S EMOTIONAL MO

Here's what we can learn from Audrey when we are hit with our own challenges.

She kept going. She rose above the situation. She didn't bad-mouth people. She didn't sit around and bitch about how Mel or Dotti or some director had mistreated her. *Boring*.

Audrey was also capable of great forgiveness. The official story is that she never saw her father again after he left her mother. Although he was rumored to be dead, Mel tracked him down through the Red Cross, and the two of them traveled to Dublin and met him in 1964. AH, in fact, remained close to her father (now married for the third time), helped support him, and sent him monthly checks for the remainder of his life (he died in 1980).

What Do Women Want?

Gentlemen, the bar has been raised—in case you (ever) find yourself wondering, "What do women want?" Here is Audrey on Rob. . . .

"He's solid in very way. I can trust him. I trust his love. I never fear I'm losing it. He reassures me. He's very loving, an affectionate man, and we like the same things—being in the country, the dogs, making trips together—and we're both avid readers, and go shopping together. *Everything* we do together is fun."

Plus—and we know you don't want to hear this, guys—Rob is also tall, handsome, conscientious (in a nice way), and great fun to share a bottle of wine with over lunch.

WOULD AUDREY . . .

Show gratitude (in spite of everything)? Absolutely. Perhaps it was the fact that she survived WWII, but Audrey was profoundly grateful for every thing that had happened in her life. In an interview with Hedda Hopper in 1953, Hedda commented that a recent *Time* magazine cover did not do her justice (and in reality, it did not), and asked her what she thought.

"I couldn't care less," Audrey replied. "I was so thrilled—it was *Time*."

See a shrink? No. It just wasn't in her background. Audrey would have had difficulty confiding her innermost thoughts to a stranger. She would have been more likely to have a girly tête-à-tête with Connie or Doris.

Engage in retail therapy? Sure. Of course, being Audrey, she could fly off to Paris or Rome and see the latest fashions.

Learn anything from her experience with men? Yes. In later years, she was asked what she had learned about men, and she replied, "Nothing—what can you learn about them? They're human beings, with all the frailties that women have. I think they're more vulnerable than women. I really do. You can hurt a man so easily."

Get bummed out? Of course she did. She's human. It is said that at the demise of her marriages, she was depressed, anxious, unhappy, and smoking three packs a day, which couldn't have helped matters.

Give up on love? No. Even though she was alone for a time, and in challenging (ahem) marriages, and even (briefly) treated shabbily by schmucks like Ben Gazzara, "I'm a romantic woman," said Audrey. "What is there without it? Life becomes just so gray." Still, she might have wondered about it a bit—when it was going to show up again—and after her two marriages, even her son Sean thought, "She might have thought it wasn't in the cards for her," but then she met Rob Wolders.

She was asked, "Did you ever think you'd fall in love again?"

"I didn't think I'd have such serenity, which is hard to come by, someone you can trust and depend on. He's absolutely there for me."

Hang in there? Absolutely. At the end of the day, Audrey kept going. After whatever disappointments she suffered, she kept them to herself, kept her chin up, and kept moving.

chapter 8

Modern Times

"Audrey loved movies, *loved* movies.
She admired her industry and was a real pro."

–Connie Wald

Audrey worked practically her whole
life, and earned her own money. Although she was a
very traditional wife, she always had her own gig, as
well as her own home in Switzerland, and her own
agent, manager, and publicist.

In studying Audrey's life, what comes through
again and again (other than her obvious talent) is how
conscientiously she worked—whether it be UNICEF,
or learning to sing for *My Fair Lady*, or dancing with
Fred Astaire in *Funny Face*. "Audrey did everything to
the best of her abilities," says Rob Wolders. "Which
were considerable."

What we see, too, is the joy she took in her work. For Audrey, it wasn't about fame, or getting a table in a good restaurant, or being on the cover of a magazine. Instead, she was very involved in the scripts she chose, and the development of her characters. Like most actors, she was always on the lookout for her next role, and had very high standards—wanting to work with the best writers, directors, costars, and camera people.

And she did.

In 1964, after the success of *My Fair Lady*, she and George Cukor were keeping their eyes open for another project to work on together. There was talk of *Oliver!*, now on the London stage, or perhaps *Peter Pan*. Audrey and Mel and baby Sean were happily ensconced in Tolochenaz (a long way from Burbank, she noted, she was spending lots of time in the nursery), but Audrey went to see the performance of *Oliver!* and wrote a very insightful assessment of the lead actress—of the entire production, in fact—that shows her intelligence and keen instincts.

Frankly, she wrote to Cukor, she found the actors' work stale, as if they had done it too often, and then followed with a five-page assessment of the entire play. She thought that the lead actress yammered too much and if *Oliver!* were ever to be made into a movie, it should be more "Dickensian, sepia, moody, and *real*."

In Audrey, we see that, in the end, it is the work that really matters. It is about being a professional, operating at your highest level. It isn't about winning *American Idol* or appearing on a reality show to become famous.

The talent comes first, of course. But after that, the work is what really matters.

A Rare (Almost) Misstep . . .

In what would have been one of the worst career moves in history (right up there with selling Manhattan to the Dutch, or turning down the chance to buy Intel stock in 1984), Mel Ferrer did not want Audrey to take the role of Holly Golightly in *Breakfast at Tiffany's*, as he was rather puritanical and did not want her to play a party girl (even if she was Givenchy clad and enjoying a chaste friendship with the then-dreamy George Peppard) Fortunately for us, Audrey said yes and went on to create one of the most iconic roles in cinematic history. Can anyone walk past Tiffany's on Fifty-seventh Street early on a spring morning without the opening lines of "Moon River" running through their mind?

We didn't think so.[27]

By the 1960s, Audrey was at the top of her game. With the critical and commercial success of a string of films, she took increasing risks, playing a nun (*The Nun's Story*), a lesbian (*The Children's Hour*), a blind woman (*Wait Until Dark*), and even, in *Breakfast at Tiffany's*, a prostitute (albeit an exceedingly well dressed one). It says something about her acting ability—or perhaps, really, her personality—that audiences accepted her in almost any role.

But while Audrey was flourishing professionally, there was trouble at La Paisible. Rumors of the Ferrers' imminent separation had been hovering around them for the past decade. Now it seemed their relationship was truly played out. Although it is impossible to guess what goes on in any relationship, part of it may have been that

---

[27] More *BAT* insider info—Steve McQueen was offered the lead male role, but turned it down and it eventually went to George Peppard. Audrey and Bullitt? Now *there* would have been a pairing.

Audrey had moved beyond Mel's opinionated manner or had grown tired of constantly trying to placate him. Surely some friction must have arisen from the reality that her career so thoroughly eclipsed his.

While she and Ferrer collaborated on several projects through the years—*Ondine* on Broadway (1954), the films *War and Peace* (1956) and *Green Mansions* (1959)—Audrey's star was clearly ascending. Alone. And although the projects Mel developed were artistically creative, they were unsuccessful at the box office—the only thing that matters in Hollywood. It must have been heartbreaking for a man of Mel's considerable ambition, talent, and drive to be known as "Mr. Audrey Hepburn."

Part of the difficulty may have also been his personality. In a business where there are few secrets, everyone loved Audrey. Her husband, on the other hand, usually merited a rolling of the eyes. "Mel was a pain in the *ass*," confided more than one person who worked with Audrey and had dealings with Mel. "He was always hanging around and meddling with the picture."

In Mel's defense, actresses in those days were not known to have a lot of "juice" in Hollywood, even those with Audrey's considerable star power. In the movie business, you needed someone in your corner. You needed an enforcer, and Mel was the enforcer.

Robert Wolders, for his part, feels Mel's contribution to Audrey's career was incalculable. "Mel guided Audrey as a husband, not as a Svengali, as some would have you think. And I think the years of her marriage coincide with the most successful years of her career."

Years later, the Wilders have their own view of Audrey's marital dilemma.

"I don't think Mel was the proper husband," observed Billy Wilder rhetorically, "but then again—who would have been the proper husband for her?"

Audrey's money was on William Holden. "Well, Bill was a nice guy. Bill would have been better—if he'd been sober."

OUR FAVORITE AUDREY MOVIE[28]

"Bitch."

"Bastard."

So ends *Two for the Road*, Audrey's most grown-up film to date.

In this Stanley Donen picture, Audrey played Joanna Wallace, the extremely chic but long-suffering wife of Mark, played by Albert Finney, an egomaniacal, absentminded architect. A thoroughly grown-up story, they are both cheating on each other. They love each other, but they also (at times) hate each other. With this final line of dialogue, Audrey closed the door on the princess, the gamine sprite, the dream.

Released in 1967, the gossamer roles of the 1950s and mid 1960s were over. The reign of the studio was also ending. Even Jack Warner would sell his beloved Warner Bros. to Seven Arts Productions in 1967. After his retirement in Palm Springs (which he hated), he surveyed the new world order: "You're nothing if you don't have a studio. Now I'm just another millionaire, and there are a lot of 'em around."

Within a year, America would be in flames. In 1968, Martin Luther King, Jr., and Robert F. Kennedy would be assassinated, with Woodstock, Altamont, Kent State, and Watergate to come.

Clearly, the world was changing.

• • •

Stanley Donen, who had started out as a Broadway hoofer in the 1940s, had directed Audrey in *Funny Face* with Fred Astaire, and in *Charade* with Cary Grant. For Audrey and her costars, these were two great experiences.

Working with Audrey was memorable for Donen, too. "Our passion has lasted through four marriages—two of hers and two of mine."

---

[28] For Henry Mancini's title track alone.

He knew that when you are on a set with someone, you get to see what they are really like.

Donen (who went on to marry three more times) said of Audrey, "Believe me, you get to know a person if you've gone through thirty-five years and three movies with her. Everyone with an important job is in an anxious, difficult, pressured situation, and it's particularly anxiety making for the lead actors. Their routine is to get up in the morning around 5:00 a.m. and put themselves on display for anyone and everyone to see, discuss, analyze, and dissect. It takes guts to go through twelve to sixteen weeks, fourteen hours a day, six days a week of the torture of having all the attention focused on you and every move you make considered, of being asked to do this on this word, go there, be ready, be sad, be happy, be funny and not become difficult.

"Audrey was fun to be with from the beginning of shooting a movie to the end."

Now Stanley had another idea for a picture—called *Two for the Road*. It would use time and travel to show the vagaries of a modern couple's marriage from courtship through boredom, success, infidelity, possible divorce, and whatever came next.

At first, Audrey was uncertain about the project. Always an instinctive actor, she knew it would ask a great deal of her emotionally, perhaps things that she did not wish to face. Mel saw its potential immediately and urged her to accept the role.

Although the script was written with her in mind, Donen knew he would be lucky to get her. He knew Audrey "was equally devoted to her acting. Her standards were high, and she was careful in choosing her parts and films." During an interview for *My Fair Lady*, a reporter asked Audrey how she chose her roles.

"It's very hard to say—I just like it, or it doesn't strike me as something I'd particularly like to do."

"Does it ever boil down to the business end of it?"

"In other words, have I ever done a picture for the money?"

"Yes—for the money."

"No, never." Audrey smiled. "Never. I've never done that. . . . I think *most* people—most performers in general—have a dream when they start a picture, and think they have something very good and sometimes the quality falls by the wayside for whatever reason. Even if they make a good picture, the audience doesn't always like it. It's a very tenuous thing, you know."

"Do you follow your instincts?" the reporter wondered. "Do you say to yourself—this is what I think, and this is what I want to do, and is the decision yours, or does anyone help you make the decision?"

"I was born with my own instincts which I try to stay true to, and so far it's made me very happy."

Finally, the reporter wondered, "Do you find it very difficult in this business to stay true to your instincts?"

No, said Audrey. "It's never been hard for me, and that's why I'm saying that humbly, that I'm saying that perhaps I'm a really fortunate person because I followed my instincts and they've brought me nothing but blessings and good fortune and kind people to work with, so so far, it's been all right."

Another factor that affected her decision was the fact that Albert Finney—who had recently made a splash in *Tom Jones*—would be her costar. Recently lauded as one of the "Angry Young Men" of British cinema, Albie (as she would come to call him) was rowdy, wild, stocky, a little uncouth, and seven years Audrey's junior. No Fred Astaire or Cary Grant smoothie, he would definitely push Audrey and wake up her image cinematically.

She decided to work with Stanley once more.

• • •

In addition to expanding her boundaries emotionally, *Two for the Road* was groove-alicious, fashionwise. Instead of her usual perfectly constructed Givenchy ensembles, Donen sent Audrey down King's Road in London with fashion coordinator Lady Claire Rendlesham to buy about thirty pieces off the rack. Audrey protested at first, but

Donen persuaded her that her character would not jet off to Paris for the couture, and to trust him. So she did, picking up mostly Mary Quant, with a dash of Hardy Amies, Michelle Posier, Paco Rabanne, and other mod designers of the day.

Although not many people knew it, Audrey and Stanley actually had a history in this regard. During *Funny Face*, when Audrey— wearing a black turtleneck, cropped black pants, and black flats— danced in the beatnik bistro, she and her director had a mild clash when she did not agree with his vision. Stanley wanted Audrey to wear white socks with the black ensemble so she would not entirely disappear in the scene. Audrey, for her part, was exceedingly self-conscious about what she considered to be her large feet. It went back and forth a bit: Audrey wanted black socks to keep the line, Stanley wanted his white socks. Finally, Stanley put his foot down (so to speak), letting Audrey know that he was the director and he wanted the white socks. He was polite about it, but at the end of the day, this was his show.

It was said that Audrey burst into tears at their disagreement— although she didn't remember it that way. At any rate, being the pro she was, she wore the socks and put everything she had into the scene (now a classic).

When she saw a final cut of the film, she sent Stanley a hand-written note: "You were right about the socks. Love, Audrey."

So instead of the careful Givenchy suits seen in *Paris When It Sizzles* or *Charade*, Audrey departed from her typical image, wearing everything from jeans and sneakers to a red and orange rugby-striped minidress with oversized acrylic sunglasses, to a black patent leather pantsuit cut so sharply, Jim Morrison would have loved it. There was a bathing suit scene that caused her great consternation at the time (not to worry—Audrey looked amazing). She even had a nude scene with Albert Finney, although, following the moviemaking dictums of the era, Finney wore white boxer shorts and a T-shirt, while Audrey kept the sheet pulled firmly up at all times, revealing about as much décolletage as a strapless evening gown.

But still, she got points for trying.

• • •

While rumors of Audrey's romances with one or another of her costars had occasionally floated about (more true on her husband's side, more untrue on hers), this time, with Albert Finney—it was the real thing.

"I love people who make me laugh. I honestly think it's the thing I like most, to laugh. It cures a multitude of ills. It's probably the most important thing in a person." And god knows, Albie and Audrey had a lot of laughs filming *Two for the Road* in France.

For his part, Finney was both discreet and honest. "We got on immediately. After the first day's rehearsals, I could tell that the relationship would work out wonderfully. Either the chemistry is there, or it isn't. . . . That happened with Audrey. During a scene with her, my mind knew I was acting but my heart didn't, and my body certainly didn't! With a woman as sexy as Audrey, you sometimes get to the edge where make-believe and reality are blurred. All that staring into each other's eyes . . .

"People are always asking me if I'm going to marry her. . . . I won't discuss it more because of the degree of intimacy involved. The time spent with Audrey is one of the closest I've ever had."

After shooting, they would duck off to little out-of-the-way cafés. Stanley Donen said that "the Audrey I saw during the making of this film I didn't even know. She overwhelmed me—she was so free, so happy. I never saw her like that, so young! I guess it was Albie."

For the first time in a long while, Audrey was happy. Of course, no matter what the gossip magazines said, she and Finney could not go too far—although separated, she and Mel were on good terms, and she did not want to do anything to jeopardize her custody of Sean.

Years later, she confided, "The most important thing is to enjoy your life—be happy—it's all that matters," and surely, this must have been something she learned during her time making *Two for the Road*.

Off the Record

A backstage story from the movie: There was a comic scene where Audrey's and Albie's characters have an argument and Albie picks her up and drops her into the pool. Although few people knew it, Audrey had a morbid fear of getting her head wet under water. Even at La Paisible, she swam in the pool with her head held way above the water. Rob remembers that he used to worry about her straining her neck.

"Can I use a double?" she asked Donen.

"Audrey, this is a scene I can't possibly shoot with a double. People have to be able to recognize it's you being thrown in."

"Well," she said. "If Albie throws me in, I may well have a heart attack."

It took three days of coaxing to get her into the pool. She was nervous about it, and Donen even poured water over her hair so she would not have to duck her head under water to get it wet. Two assistant directors were in the pool outside of camera range the entire time, in case Audrey (somehow) got into trouble.

Roll tape.

The two ADs, cognizant, perhaps, that they were responsible for the well-being of one of the most beloved women in the world, mistimed their dive into the water to rescue a sputtering Audrey Hepburn, and the scene had to be redone.

But still, even with days like that, *Two for the Road* was a blast for Audrey.

When *Two for the Road* opened at Radio City Music Hall on April 27, 1967, to ecstatic reviews, many felt that it was her best performance in years, perhaps ever—and Henry Mancini's theme will break your heart (in a good way). If you have never heard its grown-up blend of sophistication, hope, and heartbreak—his best since "Moon River"—you owe it to yourself to download it onto your iPod pronto.

For her part, Audrey Wilder also considered *Two for the Road* one of Audrey's best.

"I was crazy about *Two for the Road* and thought she really let her defenses down in it. That was a real person. She let herself be seen in not the best light. . . . Actresses all try to protect themselves usually. That's the nature of the beast. But she's really real in that."

Unfortunately, neither their best intentions nor Audrey's success were enough to keep the relationship with Mel together. While Audrey attempted to make the relationship work for the sake of her six-year-old son, Sean, their union ultimately ended. Having been married thirteen years, suffering four miscarriages and increasing tensions between their careers, Ferrer and Hepburn announced their intention to divorce on September 1, 1967.

AUDREY ON AUDREY

Unlike most actors (including her husband Mel), Audrey hated talking about herself. Hated hated *hated* it. But she was always most grateful to have been able to make a living as an actress. And she was most grateful for it all. At a salute in her honor at Lincoln Center in 1991, she said:

"As a child, I was taught that it was bad manners to bring attention to yourself. And to never, ever make a spectacle of yourself. I then went on to make a rather nice living doing just that, with a bit of

MATCH THE AUDREY FAN WITH THEIR FAVORITE AH MOVIE

> *Breakfast at Tiffany's*   *Funny Face*
> *Two for the Road*   *Wait Until Dark*
> *Roman Holiday*   *Charade*

Ralph Lauren. "In every movie I have ever watched, starting with _____, I was in love with Audrey Hepburn. I played every part! I was Gregory Peck a long time ago! I was Bill Holden, I was Cary Grant, I was her biggest fan, and am her biggest fan."

Michael Kors. "I'm a New York boy, born and bred—has to be _____, any time."

Jeffrey Banks. Also introduced Isaac Mizrahi to _____, as he had never seen it before. "*Isaac*—how can you call yourself a designer!" he (understandably) rebuked him. For anyone familiar with Mizrahi's design career since 1987, he has more than made up for his early inattentiveness.

Candy Pratts Price. _____, because she rides a Vespa, she drinks, she wears men's PJs—lots of liberation in one day!"

Andy Spade. _____; "When we were younger, my wife definitely reminded me of Audrey."

ANSWERS:

Ralph Lauren, *Roman Holiday*; Michael Kors, *Breakfast at Tiffany's*; Jeffrey Banks, *Funny Face*; Candy Pratts Price, *Roman Holiday*; Andy Spade, *Breakfast at Tiffany's*.

a hand from the greatest directors, the best writers, the most fabulous stars, glorious photography, super clothes, terrific scores, and the finest technicians in the industry. My job was to be on time and know my lines. I must say, looking at those film clips just now, I am more than ever awed and overwhelmed, at the monumental talent it's been my great great privilege to work for, and with. There's no way I can thank this beautiful evening, without thanking all of them. For finally, it is they who helped and honed, triggered and taught and pushed and pulled and dressed and photographed, guided and nurtured a totally unknown, insecure, inexperienced, skinny broad, and turned her into a marketable commodity!

"I am proud to have been in a business that gives pleasure, creates beauty and awakens our conscience, arouses compassion and perhaps most importantly, gives millions a respite from our so violent world."

"Film was her medium. It could detect her subtle feelings as well as her bursts of joy and sadness, and all the shades in between." –Stanley Donen

---

AUDREY TAKES CARE OF BUSINESS

Audrey lived well. She had created, as Connie Wald says, "a beautiful life." She had an amazing home in Switzerland, designer clothes, Frette sheets, help, and an Audi (if any of this matters to you). But she also—and this is the very cool AH dichotomy—watched her finances, was not profligate, and definitely took care of the bottom line. Like many of us, her marriages did not last forever, so she was largely responsible for taking care of her two boys, as well as helping out her parents.

And not to put too fine a point on it—because this whole conversation would probably *kill* Audrey because she was so private—while Audrey was truly "famous" and an Oscar winner, she was a movie star in the time before actresses got $29 million a picture. Still, she was very well paid for what she did—along with Elizabeth Taylor, she was the highest-paid actress of her era. And her agent, Kurt Frings, negotiated some very good deals for her. So while Audrey lived the high life when she was a globe-trotting actress, at the end of her life, she scaled back and flew coach when traveling for UNICEF.

As a single working mother for much of her adult life, Audrey was very good with money. She owned her own home and had some very good annuities to take care of the bottom line for both herself and her family.

• • •

So whether we are single or married, working or raising a family (or, most likely, both), here are some AH Money Tips from one of the most Audrey-esque women we know, Mellody Hobson, President of Ariel Capital Management, LLC.

Clip them. Save them. Study them. Put them on your bathroom mirror, if you must, but pay attention.

THE GOSPEL ACCORDING TO MELLODY

1. "Make sure that you know where the money is. I say that to women who are married because often they make their biggest financial decisions in times of great emotional distress—death or divorce. Know the account numbers, know the contact information for your financial institutions."

2. "If you are married, always maintain some form of financial independence—that might be one credit card, one banking account. This allows you to maintain your own credit history, so that if you had to re-establish it on your own, you could do it. So just one thing. It's not about separate, it's about making sure that you have some form of a financial identity that's separate from your spouse."

3. "If you're not married, I use this example that I heard from Judy Collins, 'As women we are raised to have rescue fantasies, and I'm here to tell you—no one is coming.' I call it the white knight syndrome, and as girls we are raised to read fairy tales, and the prince will come, and I always say lead your life as if there's no prince, and that way you'll be prepared and you'll have a safety net.

"A lot of women delay saving and investing, thinking, 'When my husband comes we'll figure it out.' Taking charge now makes a huge difference and gives you financial independence regardless of the outcome."

Hobson believes that "as women we are caretakers and nurturers by nature. Because of that, when it comes to thinking of our own retirement and financial security, our first thought is always to put others first, particularly our children.

"If it's a question of you funding your retirement or Jimmy going to camp, you're going to want Jimmy to go to camp, right? The big dilemma that a lot of women have is—especially single moms—do I save for my retirement, or do I save for my kid's college education, and the example that I give is that when you're on an airplane and you hit turbulence and the oxygen mask drops, they say, 'Put yourself first, and then help the person next to you.'

"The same is true when thinking about your financial future; you have to save for your retirement first, and then you can think about your children's education next because at twenty-two, you are infinitely more capable of getting out of debt if you've got college loans, than at eighty-five."

Financially, Audrey took care of business (and then some), and this is information we can all use today.

JUST WHO *IS* . . . VERY AUDREY?

"I never think of myself as an icon. What is in other people's minds is not in my mind. I just do my thing."–AH

Describing someone or something as "very Audrey" is a fashionista's way of saying extremely cool. In this very singular (and very debatable) list we've got the women and even the men who have Audrey Style. While we don't begrudge anyone for skipping ahead to see if they've made the list, we look forward to the inevitable fisticuffs at *Vogue*.

While no one can beat Audrey in the gamine department—for style, intelligence, generosity, and historical cognizance (with bonus points for her ability to rock the short haircut), Natalie Portman is our personal number-one contender for Most Audrey-esque. But recognizing that we also have to live in the real world . . . is there anyone, really, who can take Miss Hepburn's place?

Designer Jeffrey Banks, a lifelong friend of Audrey's, would say no. "There is only one Audrey, and there will *always* only be one Audrey—ever!" But a girl's got to dream, right? So if we had to choose some Audrey-esque Gals We Love . . .

Natalie Portman	Liv Tyler (current face of Givenchy, who also owns Audrey's LV makeup case)	Annette de la Renta	Margaret Curtis
Cate Blanchett		Vera Wang	Tiffany Dubin
Thandie Newton		Tanya Lewis Lee	Eva Jeanbart-Lorenzotti
Maya Lin	Jessica Yaffa	Amy Sacco	Iman
Caroline Kennedy	Twyla Tharp	Penelope Cruz	Amy Fine Collins
Selma Blair	Marguerite Marino	Scarlett Johansson	Isabel Toledo
Victoria Brynner	Uma Thurman	Mellody Hobson	Visually and aesthetically, practically every female on the islands of Japan
Veronica Webb	Virginia Mailman	Pamela Needham	
Gina de Givenchy	Diana Taylor	Carolina Herrera, Jr.	
Audrey Wilder	Sarah Jessica Parker	Zoe R. Cassavetes	Pamela Fiori
Christy Turlington	Marina Rust	Victoria Haas	Marjorie Gubelmann
Lavinia Currier	Jane Bay	Aerin Lauder	Oprah Winfrey
Susan Fales-Hill	L'Wren Scott	Emily Rossum	Susan Dell
Kate Mara	Courtney Haas	Jane Goodall	Linn Tanzman
Margaret Betts	Naomi Judd	Natalia Vodianova	Evelyn McGee-Colbert
Nicole Kidman	Inès de la Fressange	Juliana Martinez	Carrie Modine
Allison Shearmur	Elizabeth Saltzman Walker	Michelle Obama	Sofia Coppola
Babs Simpson	Reese Witherspoon	Jodie Foster	Amanda Ross
Cecilia Peck	Keilana Smith	Connie Wald	Minnie Mortimer Gaghan
Tiffany A. Stone	Paige Storment	Lauren duPont	Kate Spade
Anne Cox Chambers	Lynn Hirschberg	Zelda Sayre	Alexandra Wilk
Amanda Burden	Deb Shriver	Tory Burch	Suri Cruise

And in the Audrey-esque Very Cool Guy Category

Cary Grant

Narcisco Rodriguez

Harry Belafonte

John Isaac

Johnny Depp, Vanessa Paradis, and all of their current and future children

Stephen Gaghan

Joe Armstrong

Mr. and Mrs. Tom Hanks

Michael Kors (only in NYC or Paris)

Peter Bacanovic

Don Cheadle

Gilles Mendel

William A. Henry III

Andy Spade

Brad Pitt (during the newly enlightened Angelina Jolie era)

Stephen T. Colbert

Graydon Carter

Danny Glover

Kenneth Cole

Joseph Montebello

Steven Spielberg

James Salter

Damon Dash and Rachel Roy

Robert F. Kennedy, Jr.

Billy Wilder

Gregory Peck

| Mel Ferrer Manqué |

Brett Ratner

So, okay, your blood is boiling (Jeffrey Banks), you agree with us or disagree. What about your third cousin, your favorite aunt, Calista Flockhart, or that girl from *Grey's Anatomy*?

Well, let us know what you think.

WOULD AUDREY . . .

Get paid top dollar? Yes. For a good decade, Audrey (along with Elizabeth Taylor) was the highest-paid actress in the world. For *My Fair Lady*, for example, she received the then staggering $1 million. Her agent arranged for seven annual payments of $142,957.00, in order to help Audrey reduce her tax liability.

Keep an eye on the details? Yes. Although she did not negoti-ate them personally, she knew the ins and outs of her contracts. In a 1953 interview with Hedda Hopper, the twenty-four-year-old actress knowledgeably discussed her contract with the ease of a William Morris pro.

When Hopper commented that she might have gotten more money if she had waited to sign with Paramount after her successful Broadway run of *Gigi*, Audrey said, "I have very good agents, if I de-serve more money, I'll get it. . . . It's a seven-picture contract, with twelve months between the financing date of one picture and the starting date of the next. I can do stage and television during the twelve months. I can do a second picture for another company, but Paramount has pre-empt rights."

Fight for creative freedom? Yes. In the Hollywood community, Audrey was known for saying "no" more than "yes." After her first suc-cess, in *Roman Holiday*, the offers poured in and she could pick and choose her projects. Over the course of her career she worked with William Wyler, Billy Wilder, Stanley Donen, and Peter Bogdano-vich, and turned down far more work than she accepted—among them, *The Diary of Anne Frank*, *Oliver Twist!*, *A Bridge Too Far*, *The Turning Point*, and even *Out of Africa* (starring Meryl Streep and Robert Redford, which won seven Academy Awards).

Watch her dailies? No. AH was the rare Hollywood actor who could not bear to watch the daily rushes of her work.

Voice her opinion? Yes. Although she was wonderfully mannered, and always cognizant of the director's role, Audrey spoke up when it counted. At an early screening of *Breakfast at Tiffany's* in San Fran-cisco, Paramount's new president decided, "Well, I'll tell you one thing, we can get rid of that damn song. . . ." (meaning "Moon River")

Audrey leaped out of her seat in a rare loss of self-control and said, "Over my dead body!"

It stayed.

Invest in real estate? Absolutely. In addition to La Paisible, she also, at various times in her life, owned a vacation place in Spain and an apartment in Gstaad. When Sean married for the first time in 1985, Audrey bought him a $375,000 house in the Hollywood Hills.

Be financially aware? Yes. During the filming of *Roman Holiday*, the producers were amazed when, at the conclusion of filming, Audrey gave them an itemized report of her daily expenses, as well as returning her unspent per diem allowance. They declined to accept it.

Appear in a commercial? If you said "no," you just lost a bet.

In 1971, Audrey made her first—and only—commercial, for a collection of wigs from a Japanese company called Varie. Shot in Rome over a two-day period, she made the astonishing amount of $100,000, which she then invested in annuities for Sean and Luca. Her contract stipulated that the four one-minute commercials would never appear outside of Japan, and so far, they have not. Nor have they ever appeared on YouTube.

Ever make a few clunkers? Yes. Although they have their fans, *Paris When It Sizzles*, *War and Peace*, and *Green Mansions* are not considered her best work. However, AH remembered *Paris When It Sizzles* as a joy to make (albeit with a convoluted and almost nonexistent script), which is why she told Sean not to "correlate the experience of making the movie with its outcome."

Mess up once in a while? Sure. When she met Cary Grant in 1962, just before she was to begin filming *Charade*, she was so nervous that she spilled a bottle of red wine on his immaculate cream-colored suit.

Grant, ever the gentleman, took his jacket off and continued with the meal. (He even encouraged Audrey to take a few deep breaths and relax.)

The next day, he sent Audrey a tin of caviar with a note telling her not to worry about it.

Director Stanley Donen, who was with them at dinner, used the scene to great comic effect in the movie, when AH accidentally smushes her ice-cream cone on the lapel of Grant's suit.

Remain professional, in spite of on-set dramas? Yes. During the making of *My Fair Lady* (which was grueling), AH was under tremendous pressure, working sixteen-hour days, trying to give the director, George Cukor, what he wanted, taking dancing and singing lessons, working with musical director André Previn to learn her singing parts (later dubbed by Marni Nixon . . . which no one had the courage to tell AH). She lost fifteen pounds from stress, George Cukor was in the midst of a battle with Cecil Beaton over his ability to photograph Audrey on set, plus a jewelry bag containing her wedding ring was stolen.

Her marriage to Mel Ferrer, rumored to be fraying for years, was also in shambles. Although set photographer Bob Willoughby recalls loud words coming from her dressing room, Audrey was nothing but positive, professional, and upbeat in front of the crew.

Have the final edit? No. In the studio system, no actors or directors had this kind of pull.

Ever take acting lessons? No. When Hedda Hopper asked if she had ever studied acting, Audrey said that she relied on her instincts. "My acting must come from the inside—there is no other place it could come from. I can't fall back on technique. It can't come from any other place."

What we saw on screen (or in her life) was Pure Audrey.

Get sold out by the *National Enquirer?* No, because frankly, there was nothing to tell. Stu Crowner, who worked with AH on *Gardens of the World*, said, "She was a bitch! [laughter] Well, what do you think! If somebody was going to do a *National Enquirer* thing, I wouldn't have a single thing to say. She took care of the crew, she nursed us, she was a friend to us, she was professional, which was the best kind of friend you could be! She was on time, she had her words down, she contributed to the script. . . . And then she looked wonderful, of course.

"She was very generous with her spirit and very generous with how you felt. In other words, she considered how you felt rather than how she felt. Maybe she took care of herself, her psyche, and her soul, and all those things, but it wasn't at the expense of her friends or colleagues."

Give it her all? Yes. As Stanley Donen recalled, "She wanted only the best and fought for it. She took her work very seriously; on the set she was always in good spirits, always on time. . . . She approached acting with determination, intelligence and a lack of selfishness I have rarely seen."

Stay loyal in the most cutthroat industry in the world? Yes. Audrey was immensely loyal. Whether in business or personal relationships, once she trusted you, that was it. (So if someone disappointed her, she felt that even more strongly.)

Audrey surrounded herself with very good people, and remained true to them for years. She stayed close friends with Billy Wilder, her director on *Sabrina* and *Love in the Afternoon*, and his wife, Audrey. She worked with directors William Wyler and Stanley Donen several times. She first met Hubert de Givenchy while filming *Sabrina*, and he went on to become the executor of her estate. Similarly, she first met her agent, Kurt Frings, and her longtime hair and makeup team during *Roman Holiday*, and stayed with them the rest of their lives.

Fire her publicist? Yes. During her marriage to Mel, he was annoyed that Givenchy used Audrey's image in an ad for a perfume he had created for her, L'Interdit, and did not pay her. Givenchy was more than willing to do so, but Audrey did not want him to, believing that that's what friends do for one another. Mel enlisted Henry Rogers, Audrey's respected publicist, to go to Paris and begin negotiations with Hubert's brother.

When Audrey learned of this, as well as a trumped-up award— Mel wanted the Cannes Film Festival to award Audrey to get her to attend—she said, "Neither of you seem to understand. I don't want anything from Hubert. I don't need his money. He is my friend. If I have helped him build his perfume business, then that's exactly what one friend should do for another. . . . Yes, I even want to walk into a drugstore and buy the perfume at the retail price."

Later that night she called Rogers, weeping. At first, he was alarmed and thought something had happened to Sean. Audrey was upset at all the backstage machinations going on around her, and the feeling that other people expected her to cash in on her friendship with Givenchy.

She said that while she valued his friendship, she could not work with him anymore. She was upset about his embarrassing her about Hubert and trying to get her to accept some phony award.

Rogers felt terrible. Here was this generous, creative creature sobbing her eyes out over the machinations of Hollywood. Part of the difficulty of working with Audrey was the fact that Audrey wanted to work less and Mel was always pushing her out there—more more more *more*. As publicist, Henry had to serve two masters and "performed a constant balancing act between Mel's insatiable desire for Audrey's new publicity, and her reluctance."

Rogers explained how he saw the situation, and his peripheral part in it, and graciously accepted Audrey's wishes. And yes, they remained friends.

chapter 9

St. Audrey

"Life's most persistent and urgent question is,
'What are you doing for others?'"

–Martin Luther King, Jr.

Audrey had enjoyed such great fortune
as an actress. Now, it was time to give back. In 1988,
she was asked to serve as Special Ambassador for the
United Nations Children's Fund. "I auditioned for this
job for forty-five years," she said, "and I finally got it."
Once it was learned that Audrey was on board, the invi-
tations poured in from around the world—"and in our
enthusiasm, we accepted all of them," says Wolders.

In the space of five years, they made more than
fifty humanitarian trips—to Japan, Turkey, Holland,
Central America, El Salvador, Vietnam, and Australia.
Long before actors like George Clooney, Brad Pitt, or
Angelina Jolie, Audrey was one of the first celebrities
to go to places like Bangladesh, Ethiopia, and Sudan.

For Audrey, her commitment to UNICEF was nothing out of the ordinary. While some might see her devotion to her work as extraordinary, she believed that "it is logic that someone who has been privileged should do something for those who are not. Again, that was the way I was brought up." In fact, Audrey believed that through her work with UNICEF, she received even more than she gave.

"It's an extraordinary thing that's happened to me. To be able to express my need to help children and to care for them in some way. I personally can do very little, but I can contribute to a whole chain of events which is UNICEF, and that's a marvelous feeling! It's like a bonus to me at the end of my life. And if this career has given me something very special, it's the fact that it's left me with whatever this is—this voice, this curiosity that people still have to see me, to talk to me—which I can use for the good of children. What could be nicer?"

And so, the third act of Audrey's life began.

For Audrey and Rob, their devotion to UNICEF was immediate and lasting. "It was twenty-four hours a day, in terms of study, preparation, the speeches, then the field trips," Rob recalls. Audrey approached her work with the attentiveness with which she used to prepare for a role; writing her own speeches at her dining room table, speaking to journalists in their native language, and when they traveled, it was just she and Rob on a transport plane—not a film crew from *Entertainment Tonight* covering their every move.

She just went out and did it. John Isaac, a UNICEF photographer and friend, said that the organization "got $1 million in contributions every time she made an appeal to Barbara Walters, or wherever. She made such a huge impression."

Isaac first met Audrey on her trip to Ethiopia in 1988. As he recalls, "We hit it off right from the beginning, and she had a terrific sense of humor, so we could joke about things, and at the same time, she was very sensitive. And she also had a very philosophical edge to her, she liked philosophy, she liked Tagore. . . . I told her I had a favorite poet, and she said that she had a favorite, too. So then we exchanged the same lines. He talks about love in a way, he talks about true friendship, true love, he says: 'May my loving you not be a burden on you, for I freely chose to love you.' And it's almost like a true love where you don't expect anything.

"Audrey was so deep and so sensitive. In no way would she want to offend anybody, even though there were people who were starving, and who were dying over there. But for her, dignity was so important." Isaac saw this firsthand when he traveled with Audrey and Rob to Bangladesh in October 1989. "Often the kids would have flies all over them, but she would just go hug them. I had never seen that. Other people had a certain amount of hesitation, but she would just grab them. Children would just come up to hold her hand, touch her— she was like the Pied Piper."

But still, among the press, there were some snipers. As Rob recalls, "When she did the UNICEF work, people would refer to her as if she were a saint, and that puzzled her and ultimately made her a little angry because people would compare her to a Mother Teresa. At the same time, one shouldn't underplay the importance that she came to have in her charitable efforts—it's remarkable in those few years, in regard to drawing attention to the plight of the children."

The Only Club Audrey Would Have Joined

While Audrey was a perennial member of any Best Dressed List anyone can conjure up (still), she was not a joiner and, other than a beach club she went to in Sardinia in the late 1960s so Sean would have a place to swim, was not a club member.

However, we think there is one club she would have joined: The Council on Foreign Relations, the influential, nonpartisan foreign policy organization founded in 1921 and housed in a former Frick mansion on Park Avenue in New York City. With politically savvy members of the East Coast aristocracy like Madeleine Albright, Tom Brokaw, Richard Holbrooke, Henry Kravis, Colin Powell, David Rockefeller, and newbie Angelina Jolie, we have no doubt she would have fit right in.

Although her contribution to UNICEF was considerable and her impact incalculable, Audrey was not exactly living in exile in Switzerland, or constantly traveling for relief efforts. Her equal priorities were her family and friends. In fact, she was so successful in her effort to raise Sean and Luca in a "normal" environment that it was only when Sean started working in the movie business in his early twenties that he realized that she "was a huge star."

AUDREY AND HER FANS . . .

One of the hallmarks of Audrey Fans is how well behaved they are. When asked how Audrey managed to make her way around major cities without the use of a bodyguard or hiding out in a Cadillac Escalade with tinted windows, Rob said, "It was really remarkable because people were so respectful of her. They would follow her. I saw people stop in their tracks in places like New York and then very shyly come up to her, and say, 'My god, you look like Audrey Hepburn!' She was so extraordinarily kind with them.

"The only time it would be bothersome," Rob recalled, "would be if we would be leaving some event, these people have some sort of underground network, they knew she was there. And there would be dozens of these people with these stacks of photographs and then I or Sean would have to curb it because they would give her ten photographs to sign."

They All Laughed. *Not.*

Although Audrey would go on to have a cameo (as an angel, natch) in Steven Spielberg's *Always,* her last starring role was in Peter Bogdanovich's wildly self-indulgent *They All Laughed.*

We are not going to recap the plot, which also stars John Ritter, Dorothy Stratten, Patti Hansen, and Ben Gazzara. While Vincent Canby panned it the first time around in *The New York Times* (not without reason, most would say), this 1981 film has gone on to become a cult favorite of directors like Quentin Tarantino and Wes Anderson.

Overlooking plot, dialogue, pacing, and an excessive use of physical sight gags (mostly on the part of Ritter), should you decide to rent it from Netflix, *They All Laughed* is worth watching if only:

1. To see Audrey walk so freely through Midtown Manhattan. And her friends are right, she walks *fast.* Not surprisingly, she looks terrific in her own wardrobe of jeans and silk shirts (note that the lining of her pea coat matches her shirt), and the occasional Burberry trench.

2. Notice how openly affectionate she is with Glenn Scarpelli (who plays Michael Niotes, her movie son). It is obvious from watching the two of them interact that she truly loves children. She is far more physically demonstrative, and comfortable, with him than with her (movie) love interest, Ben Gazzara.

3. In addition to working as Bogdanovich's personal assistant, Sean makes an appearance as a slightly uncomprehending Latin (or is he an Italian?) playboy. It is easy to see why Audrey was so proud of him.

4. To see late 1970s New York City in all of its gritty, pre-cleaned-up tourist-era glory. For the roller disco, women's (and men's) fashions, the World Trade Center, downtown when it was still downtown, and characters' propensity to casually share joints and/or pick up members of the opposite sex: priceless. Oh, and everybody smokes constantly throughout the entire movie.

5. Well, she did earn $1 million for six weeks' work, with a generous expense account.

6. Audrey had her first real "date" (although they would not have called it that) with Robert Wolders at this time.

If her eyes are a bit sadder, a bit more knowing than when we first saw her in *Roman Holiday*, Audrey has lost none of her beauty. If anything, her knowledge of the ways of the world make us care for her even more. Still, as much as we love her—and her work—our Audrey is ill-served by the entire endeavor.

AUDREY AND ROB: THE INSIDE STORY

Rob had always felt that he and Audrey were fated to meet.

They were so similar in their thoughtfulness, their low-key-ness (so un American), their attention to detail and quiet good charm. If you ever wonder what Audrey must have been like, meet Rob.

As he says of their relationship, "We had the good fortune to find each other, and I had gone through some bad stuff as well. We had no friction or hardships, really, except for some of the petty things which were easily settled."

In addition to her intelligence, generosity of spirit, and obvious beauty (which Rob swears Audrey did not really see in herself), what Rob also loved about Audrey were her "moments of glad grace." She could be dignified when the moment called for it, but also loved to joke around. Rob says that "when she got older and she would be clowning around with kids in the field or if a meeting got too serious, she would lighten up the situation, and several times she would say to me, 'I really can't behave like this at my age, can I?' and I would always encourage her to not change.

"She was full of beans, full of fun, full of mischief, and didn't think that she had a superior quality. Which is interesting, you presume that people who project glamour and confidence, security, that they have perhaps always had it, or that they arrived at it and take it for granted. With Audrey, that was never the case."

One of Our Favorite 1980s AH Quotes

"This chocolate is so good, I could rub it in my hair!"

–Audrey, to Rob

WHAT AUDREY AND OPRAH
HAVE IN COMMON

Long before Oprah had to answer the tiresome (and far from original) "Why aren't you married?" question, Audrey had to deal with it in the press again.

And again.

And again.

Even Barbara Walters got into the act, asking if—or when—she and Rob planned to marry. "We are married," Audrey answered, "just not formally." She also quoted one of Billy Wilder's lines: "If you have a winning combination—you don't fool with it! So I'm not going to fool with anything! We're very happy this way—we don't need marriage!"

Besides, Rob always believed that the end of each of her marriages was so harrowing for someone as finely tuned as Audrey that he never would have dreamed of putting her through that. It would be, he said, "like dragging someone back to the electric chair and making her sit down again." Much as he loved her—and she him—it would never happen.

The Golden Boy: The Update

Audrey's divorce from Mel was so emotionally traumatic that she only saw him twice afterward—at Sean's graduation and first wedding. (And this from a woman who was able to forgive and support her Nazi-inclined father, who deserted her and her mother on the eve of World War II). She remained friends with Andrea, mainly for Luca's sake. But what of Bill Holden, the Golden Boy?

Personally, things did not turn out so well for him. After his early success in Hollywood, Bill Holden lost energy in his middle years, appearing in mostly lackluster films and not seeming to care all that much about acting. In 1966, his drinking took a darker turn when he was involved in a car accident in Italy in which the other driver was killed. It was determined that Holden had been driving under the influence of alcohol. He was charged with vehicular manslaughter and received an eight-month suspended prison sentence.

While appearing in movies such as *The Wild Bunch, The Towering Inferno,* and an Oscar-nominated performance in *Network* in the 1970s, he devoted most of his time to wildlife preservation at his animal preserve in Africa. His longtime relationship with actress Stephanie Powers sparked his interest in animal welfare.

Holden died a dozen years before Audrey, in 1981, as a result of a fall in his high-rise apartment in Santa Monica, California. Drunk and alone when he slipped on a throw rug, he was not found for four days. His body was cremated and his ashes were scattered in the Pacific Ocean. After his death, Stephanie Powers became a director of the Mount Kenya Game Ranch and president of the William Holden Wildlife Foundation, whose work continues to this day.

Bob Willoughby, who knew both Audrey and Bill, once remarked, "Everyone was in love with Audrey, but no one more than Bill."

ADD STEVEN SPIELBERG
TO THE LIST, TOO

In 1988, Audrey shot a cameo in Steven Spielberg's *Always*. She and Rob were hesitant to accept the part—she plays a sort of heavenly angel in white trousers and a ribbed sweater who advises a character played by Richard Dreyfuss—since they had been doing some very hard traveling for UNICEF for the past four or five months, but she did (fortunately for us).

Rob recalls that Audrey needed a break, and was reluctant to do it, but they were flown out to Montana and the production company had provided a beautiful house in the woods for them, and they had an entire week before they were needed on set, so it was almost like a holiday for them. Rob remembers that Audrey was embarrassed, too, by all the adulation from Spielberg, that most knowledgeable of directors—"They treated her like some sort of a deity," says Rob.

When it was time for her to be on the set, they did not want her white costume to get even the slightest smudge (her "heaven" was a burned-out forest), so the grips put her in a chair, picked her up, and carried her to her key light, much to her delight and chagrin. "She had a great time," Rob recalls. "She adored Steven."

From a career that began in 1951, it was her last film role.

"I found her a singular person. Unique is a very overused word, but she was unique–there was no one like her before, and there's been no one like her since."

–Gregory Peck

AH'S LIKES AND DISLIKES
(YES, SHE HAD THEM)

For someone with the reputation of being so, well, *saintly*, there really were a few things Audrey hated. And loved.

| AH Loved |

Her two sons

Dark chocolate

Cigs (after her English brand was discontinued,
she smoked Kent or Parliament)

Hubert de Givenchy: the clothes, the parfum, and the man

To laugh

Dogs

Winter

The color white

Afternoon naps

Her ~~overbearing~~ well-meaning mother

The occasional Scotch
(J&B neat, no more than a finger, after 6:00 p.m.)

Raspberry preserves

The kind gesture

UNICEF

Pasta en famille with Connie Wald

Robbie

| AH Hated |

Garlic

Red flowers

Prejudice

Unkindness

Violent movies

Thinking about the past

Formal exercise

Talking about herself

Small-minded people

Watching her old movies

Good-byes

| AH Was Afraid Of |

Getting her head dunked under water

WOULD AUDREY . . .

Get a tattoo, piercings, have a page on MySpace? Come *on* . . . Audrey did not even have her ears pierced.

Visit a strip club? Actually, she did. Sort of. If visiting the famed burlesque show at the Crazy Horse in Paris counts. In 1959, Henry Wolf, the legendary art director of *Harper's Bazaar*, traveled with Richard Avedon to do a cover shoot with Audrey, Mel, Buster Keaton, and Art Buchwald. Avedon took the main shots, but Henry shot a ton of backstage stuff.

One night, he took her to Crazy Horse at her request. He called to get a table and they said, no, they did not have any. He then asked, "Would you have a table for Audrey Hepburn?" and of course they did. The show began, and one of the dancers came right up to the table, not recognizing Audrey, and when she did, nearly dropped her fans.

Stand on ceremony? No. When she visited the UN, the directors always wanted to have lunch with her and she said, no, she wanted to have lunch with her friend, the UN photographer who accompanied her on her trips abroad, John Isaac. Being the "low man on the totem pole" (in Isaac's words), John was visited by a director who said he could not accept, because the directors would be upset.

John told Audrey that they would get together after work. "Why, are you busy?" she wondered, and he said no, and after he explained the situation, she said, "Bullshit, you will be my escort!"

So they went to lunch together at the UN dining room. "I was her friend, and that was it," Isaac recalled.

Consider herself a superwoman? No way. Just so we don't leave you with the impression that Audrey was some sort of a Superwoman who had everything under control at all times, in a letter to her father's wife, Fidelma, in July 1980, she confides that her marriage to Andrea is in bad shape, and she is suffering but keeping her head up and keeping going. "I am very torn about this, but I can only do the best I can."

Tone it down, style-wise? Yes. Even though Audrey was—and even today, continues to be—a style icon, she took her role lightly. She loved clothing, but when her life became less public, she was just as happy dressing casually. Rob recalled that "Audrey was in jeans 80 percent of the time. She wore ballet-type slippers, always. On occasion, sandals or clogs in case she had to step into the garden. A Lacoste shirt, no belt. She didn't like belts, except on dresses, but on jeans, never."

Use creative fund-raising techniques? Yes. Early on during her time at UNICEF, Audrey contributed a painting that she had done of an Ethiopian woman with a single tear. It was sold at auction for $12,000, which bought three camels that were used to carry vaccines for children to Chad in Central Africa.

"Get" it? Yes. Kevin Aucoin did her makeup on numerous occasions. The first time was when Richard Avedon shot her for a Revlon ad, and later when she got the Lincoln Center Film Society Award in 1991. As Kevin recalled, "She was very empathetic. There is a quality about her that is hard to put words to . . . she was, of course, really smart and very discerning, so she had this amazing combination that made it sort of unbelievable."

Kevin began talking to her about gay teen suicide and "she *got* it. You could really talk to her. She was very in touch and very aware."

Working with her was one of the great experiences of his life, and he thought "she had a really engaging presence that manifested itself in truth coming through her eyes. She was very there, you got her full attention. When you were talking to her, she was talking to you alone. And if she was talking about the flowers you sent, she was talking about them alone. And you knew she meant what she said."

Know when to leave the stage?

Yes. Unlike so many actors, she knew when to shift gears. According to Candy Pratts Price, "Audrey disappeared at the right time. Having a private life is key. And I think what we're dealing with so much now is so many of these girls are not private, and never leaving. Audrey knew when to leave the party— you've got to arrive at the right time, and you've got to leave at the right time.

"And I think *reserve*. I think that's the main thing—stay out of the damn party! She must have been worshipped by the man she was with because she did not need to sit at the banquette at El Morocco."

But needless to say, given her talent, Audrey was always inundated with film offers and possible projects. After the success of *Roman Holiday*, she admitted, the offers came pouring in. At the time of Audrey's death, Julia Roberts was still looking for a project they could work on together.

Be politically radical?

Yes, in her own way. "I am filled with a rage at ourselves!" she told Larry King. "I don't believe in collective guilt, but I do believe in collective responsibility." She was invited to have an audience with Pope John Paul II, but she declined, as she disagreed with the Catholic Church's teachings on birth control. Having traveled through Central America and Africa, she had seen the downside of such beliefs.

Speaking to a group of U.S. senators, she said, "We study war. Why can't we study and have a science of peace?"

Follow her instincts? Yes, always. Audrey was a holistic person — turning her back on Hollywood, leaving her marriages (painful as that was) when they were no longer good for her, doing what she thought best for herself and her family — and now, it seemed her life was where she dreamed it might be. Her sons brought her great joy. She had challenging work that she loved and rewarded her. She had a beautiful home, and a true partner. There were challenges, yes, but she moved ahead with things and did the best she could.

Have been able to do her UNICEF work without Rob's extremely able assistance? No.

Keep it together? Yes. Cynthia Rowley noticed this, too. "I also love that Audrey stayed with it her whole life, she didn't give up. Crisp shirt, little flats, or a sleeveless shell. People are like, oh no, I can't wear sleeveless, my arms are too . . . she was like sixty and she's still wearing sleeveless tops."

Consider herself a saint? No. Way. (Although we might.) Actually, the whole "saint" thing makes her less than human — by putting her up on a pedestal and making her better than us, Audrey is dehumanized, and this lessens her inherent coolness. While her work for UNICEF (as a private citizen) went far beyond the bounds of mere charity, she was also a normal person — she smoked, drank Scotch, let her dogs sleep on the bed, got lonely once in a while, stayed at five-star hotels, and got into the occasional tiff with her mother.

Write her autobiography? No, although the legendary agent Irving "Swifty" Lazar wrote her three-page, single-spaced letters beseeching her to do so, and Jacqueline Kennedy Onassis regularly called her at home in Switzerland to also try to persuade her.

Audrey turned everyone down, mainly because she was too busy living her life in the present, but also, any decent life story, she knew,

would have to involve other people, and she had no interest in betray-
ing (as she saw it) others' confidences.

Her son Sean wrote a beautiful photo-memoir about his mother's
life, *Audrey Hepburn, An Elegant Spirit* (Atria Books, 2003). AH
would have been pleased.

chapter 10

Legend

"I don't know how long we last in people's
memories, but if anyone has the right to be
remembered, she does."–Blake Edwards

In September 1992, Audrey and Rob
went to Somalia for UNICEF. It was hell, unimagina-
ble. Beyond anything she had ever seen. There were
so many graves, and so many dead. For once, it was
almost too much.

"I walked into a nightmare," Audrey said. "I have
seen famine in Ethiopia and Bangladesh, but I have
seen nothing like this—so much worse than I could
have possibly imagined. I wasn't prepared for this."

Upon their return, there was worse news. Audrey
had been complaining of severe stomach pain. At first,
the doctors thought it might be some sort of a virus.
After extensive tests at Cedars-Sinai Medical Center in
Los Angeles, they learned it was cancer, that dreaded
fraternity.

Now, remembering the time before Audrey's death is troubling for Rob. "When Audrey became ill, I asked her—this was a few months before the end—'What if we had just spent the years that we had been fortunate enough to be together? If we had spent those years here, in Switzerland, to be together with the dogs, with the family,' and it's one of the few times that she was quite angry with me, because it indicated a certain selfishness, and she said, 'think of all we would have missed.'"

But nevertheless, admits Rob, "if I were to know for certain that the UNICEF work, which might have taken away from her years, from her life, I would not hesitate to give all that up, just so she would be with us longer.

"We had a blessed fourteen years, but when it is taken away, you suffer all the more, because it was that good. We had no friction or hardships, really, except for some of the petty things, which were easily settled. Whatever shortcomings either one of us had—she had very few, I had many—she accepted. She made people better, and she would bring out the best in people. There was just no way of being mean with Audrey—even today, you know? People are hard put to say something bad about her."

• • •

Her sons made the decision not to tell Audrey the extent of her prognosis. In 1988, she and John Isaac had had a conversation about who had the right to life. As Isaac recalls, "She asked me and I said I think I have the right to my own life, and I said I don't want to be hanging on to some tube. She said, 'Exactly, John, that's exactly what I think.'

"Robbie called and also Sean wanted to know, when they made the decision they asked me. That's why she went in a dignified way."

In retrospect, Rob realizes that might have been a mistake. "Neither the boys nor I would acknowledge that she was actually dying. We couldn't imagine that she could—she was too precious. And we made a mistake in not letting her know how ill she was. In retrospect, I think that was very unfair to her because she was as realistic about death as she was about life. When she began to sense what was happening, she made us promise that we would let her go when she would indicate that it was time. We promised to do that, but I don't think we really followed through."

With the realization of those forced to remain behind, he admitted, "We were begging for every minute, really." Audrey's unexpected illness affected Rob greatly, perhaps in ways, even now, he is barely aware of. "She was so extraordinarily giving and compassionate. She gave me a great deal of self worth. Subsequently, I had a great sense of failure when she died, because she made me feel that I could protect her. She entrusted herself to me."

Thanks to the intervention of Hubert, Audrey, Rob, and the boys were able to borrow Bunny Mellon's plane and fly from Los Angeles to Switzerland. They spent their last Christmas together with a few close friends, such as Hubert, visiting. "I'm so glad I'm home," Audrey said. "I can see my trees again."

It was a terrible time. It was a beautiful time, too, to have these weeks together. As Sean recalled, "We were, of course, shocked and dismayed and horrified and angry, and she said no, death is just a part of life. It's just another phase of life. And she made peace with things. We had a wonderful opportunity to say to each other all the things you want to be able to share with someone when you know they're not going to be there. I think she felt that her last Christmas was her best Christmas because, I can't tell you exactly why, she felt at that time. We were all around her, we were there for the right reasons. And she said she was now sure that we really loved her."

During one of her last conversations with Sean, he asked her— did she regret anything?

"I do regret something," she said, "I regret not meeting the Dalai Lama. He is probably the closest thing to God we have on this earth. So much humor . . . so much compassion . . . humanity."

Audrey died at home in Tolochenaz, Switzerland, on January 20, 1993. She was sixty-three years old.

Years earlier, she had reflected on her life, "If my world were to cave in tomorrow, I would look back on all the pleasures, excitements and worthwhilenesses I have been lucky enough to have had. Not the sadness, not my miscarriages or my father leaving home, but the joy of everything else. It will have been enough."

Once, commenting on her own possible legacy, Audrey said simply, "I do my best. I wish I could do more." While Rob knew that "if there is anything she would have wished for, it is that her work be continued."

"I think people love her off the screen for the same reason they love her performances–a kind of orderliness and formality."–William Holden

---

Audrey Life Lessons

Never Complain, never explain.

Audrey was not a whiner. When things were stressful during the filming of *My Fair Lady*, when Mel was being his usual pain-in-the-neck self, when her wedding ring was stolen from her dressing room, when her mother was cross with her—she didn't complain. She kept her head down and got on with it.

Conserve your energy for the important things.

Every once in a while, spend the day in bed to rest up between gigs. In his later years, Picasso had enormous energy. What most people don't know is, he spent one day in bed, resting, and one day up and about. Along with the occasional nap, Audrey made a point of conserving her energy between film jobs.

Don't be a whiner.

When she was diagnosed with cancer Audrey did not say, "Why me?" She thought death was as natural as life.

Celebrate her birthday.

May 4 was Audrey's birthday, and while Elvis fans practically make a national holiday out of Elvis's birthday, why not remember Audrey in your own way? Now, we're not saying make a pilgrimage to Tolochenaz, or turn La Paisible into Graceland, but here are a few things you can do to let AH know you are thinking of her.

Throw a party.

Make a contribution to UNICEF. It can be just a few dollars, but give what you feel comfortable doing.

Have (liquid) breakfast at Tiffany's. Okay, we totally made this up—as Audrey preferred J&B Scotch (but Holly Golightly loved her champers). Here is a delicious drink from our favorite mixologist, Dale DeGroff, author of *The Craft of the Cocktail*.

Miss Golightly's Champagne Passion

1 ounce Cointreau
1 ounce passion fruit puree
4 ounces Champagne

Assemble the Cointreau and the passion fruit puree in a cocktail shaker and shake well with ice. Strain into a Champagne flute. Fill slowly and carefully with cold Champagne. Garnish with a thin spiral of orange peel twisted over the top of the drink, then dropped it into the drink.

Buy back her personal letters. Audrey's letters are occasionally sold by former "friends" and in-laws. (Relatives, we might add, that she was very kind to during their lives.) For major, major bonus points in Audrey World and all-around good Karma, buy them and return them to Sean or Rob.

Have fun with it all.

Audrey was never afraid to have a little fun at her own expense. Connie Wald tells the story, "I remember once she stopped at Tiffany's in L.A., and was going to San Francisco and ordered something and wanted to pick it up, and they said to her, 'Have you any identification?' And she smiled at them and said, 'My face!'"

Some of Audrey's Nicknames

AH was generally known as Audrey, Mrs. Ferrer, Mrs. Dotti, or, if she was on a film set, Miss Hepburn. But among favored friends, she also had a few nicknames. . . .

Aud—English chumminess favored by Peter O'Toole in *How to Steal a Million*. A very happy set, on which she called him Gov.

Monkey Puzzle, or MP—the nickname her father gave her as a child. He was the only person to call her this.

Dad—While writing from the Beverly Hills Hotel in 1957, she signed letters to Fred Zinnemann, her director on *The Nun's Story*, this way. Inexplicable, but true.

| An Exceedingly Arbitrary Audrey List |

Herewith, an updated list of some things AH would have loved.

Chocolate? Scharffen Berger, Swiss baking chocolate

Bathing suit? Eres

Hotels? Beverly Hills Hotel, Plaza Athénée (New York/Paris), Raphael (Paris), Claridge's (London)

Shoes? Ferragamo (still), Manolo Blahnik, Keds, Roger Vivier, possibly Belgian loafers

Leggings? Danskin

THE AUDREY QUESTIONNAIRE

Favorite color? White

Favorite color for evening wear? Black or red. Solid colors, no flowers, prints, or ruffles, except the one time she wore a beautiful Givenchy-designed, pink sari-style evening dress, when she substituted for Mother Teresa as a presenter at the 1992 Oscars.

Ice cream? Chocolate

Treat? Baking chocolate

Movie? In later years, *Witness*, *Ferris Bueller's Day Off*, *E.T.*, and *The Princess Bride* (she also had the sound track). But in general, Audrey didn't talk about films, let alone her own.

Favorite poem? According to Gregory Peck, it was "Unending Love," by Indian poet Rabindranath Tagore.

Favorite actress? Anything with Michelle Pfeiffer, Meryl Streep, Cher, or Julia Roberts in it

Music? According to Rob, "Audrey liked well-ordered music. She liked Bach very much, but found it difficult to have music on unless she could sit and listen to it. She loved jazz and George Shearing's music."

Public figure most admired? Gandhi and the Dalai Lama

Guilty pleasure? She loved American television shows. Living in Switzerland especially in the early years, they could not get them, but Robert Wolders's sister lived in Holland, where they got the programs, and they used to send tapes. Audrey said that "*L.A. Law* was so wonderful because the ensemble acting between the people is so good. Only in America would people have the opportunity to really develop a character because they work with the same people day in and out." Audrey also got a kick out of watching *Dynasty*.

Favorite authors? Graham Greene, Tom Wolfe, Jeffrey Archer, Willa Cather, Lawrence Sanders. In her twenties, she loved Rudyard Kipling's work. Although she spoke several languages—English, Dutch, French, Italian, and Spanish—and wrote notes to Hubert in French, she read in English for relaxation.

During the UNICEF years, she didn't have much time to read because she was always trying to keep up to date with the UN publications and the reports from the field.

Politics? Became more involved with politics because of UN work. Robert Wolders believes "she had always been political to a great extent."

Favorite artist? El Greco, Mary Cassatt. The bulk of the paintings in her home were by Bob Kane. Audrey also drew and sketched beautifully herself.

Two things that would surprise us about Audrey? "She had great legs!" laughs Bob Willoughby. Audrey also loved shopping malls; that was the first thing she wanted to do when she visited Rob's family in Rochester. She loved the concept of it, and she liked to buy gifts for friends that you could not get in Europe. She loved the Gap to buy baby clothes because the Gap did not exist in Europe then.

Personal philosophy? "Childishly optimistic." Audrey always felt that everything would be all right at the end.

Ballet flats? Capezio, Repetto, or Delman (black only)

Magazine subscriptions? *Foreign Affairs* (publication of the Council on Foreign Relations), French and British *Vogue, Vanity Fair, Cook's Illustrated, British House and Garden, Town & Country,* O magazine

The "a girl's gotta dream" catalog? Vivre, Van Cleef & Arpels, L.L. Bean (for doggy canine accoutrements), Williams-Sonoma

Scotch? J&B or Chivas Regal Black Label

Favorite movie (her own)? *The Nun's Story.* Audrey was understandably proud of the work she did on this 1959 film. Even today, Rob can barely watch it, he finds the acting so close to the real Audrey. (And for the record, Audrey Wilder thinks that *Two for the Road* is AH's "most honest" work as an actress.)

Christmas cards? UNICEF

Watch? Didn't wear one

Pocketbook? Pocketbooks were not the overblown status symbols they are today, but AH favored Hermès or, in the 1970s, LV's Speedy 30, when walking with Givenchy in Paris.

AUDREY ADDRESSES

| New York City |

57th Street and Fifth Avenue. In terms of style, this is *it* for Audrey World—the epicenter of all things Hepburn-esque. On one corner you have Tiffany, on the other, Bulgari, where Audrey got her (second) engagement ring, then Bergdorf Goodman, Van Cleef & Arpels, and Louis Vuitton.

Tiffany & Co. Although you can now buy Tiff Co. bibelots world-wide or on the Web, the 57th Street store is still the granddaddy of them all. Wake up very early, grab your Ray-Bans, Danish, and New York coffee and sashay down to Fifth Avenue and have your Holly Golightly moment. www.tiffany.com

Taffin Jeweler's. Hubert is, sadly, no longer designing for the house he founded, but his nephew, James, has picked up the family's style standard and designs the most beautiful jewelry. Stop by, say hello, and spring for some scented candles. By appointment only, and by the way—Audrey would have loved his work. Now you can, too. 685 Fifth Avenue, 10th floor; 212-421-6222; www.Taffin.com

Roger Vivier. Add some *belle de jour* to your life—with locations in New York, London, and Paris. If it's good enough for Catherine Deneuve, Ava Gardner, Queen Elizabeth II, the Beatles, Audrey, and Inès de la Fressange, surely it's good enough for you. 750 Madison Avenue at 65th Street; 212–861–5371; www.rogervivier.com

Ferragamo. AH's favorite shoe master. Locations throughout the world. When in Florence, make a pilgrimage to the house's (sigh) shoe museum. www.salvatoreferragamo.it

Pierre Hotel. On their first date, Audrey and Rob met for drinks at the Pierre. Years later, at a photo shoot for *New York* magazine, she had forgotten her earrings, said, "Excuse me," and went downstairs to borrow a pair from Bulgari. A very large man accompanied her to make sure they were safe. 2 East 61st Street; www.tajhotels.com/pierre

Plaza Athénée. One of Audrey's favorite hotels in NYC or Paris. For you younger television mavens, Sarah Jessica Parker stayed at the Paris outpost with Baryshnikov during their romance on *Sex and the City*. NYC: 37 East 64th Street; 212-734-9100; www.plaza-athenee .com. Paris: 25 Avenue Montaigne; www.plaza-athenee-paris.com

T. Anthony Luggage. Old school. A favorite of the Duke and Duchess of Windsor, WASPs, and Hollywood royalty alike. Although made of canvas, it wears like iron. *Vogue* editors favor the very purple-ish blue. Don't forget your monogram. 445 Park Avenue; 212-750-9797. www.tanthony.com

Tracy Feith. Face it: Audrey had fabulous legs her entire life, and although she worried that her Ralph Lauren dress was riding too high when she raised her arms for a shoot with Steven Meisel and the boys for *Vanity Fair*, she looked perfect. When she temporarily put Givenchy away and wore some of the younger designers during her *Two for the Road* days, Tracy Feith would have been perfect. Young young young young. She had said good-bye to grumpy Mel and was being wooed by an Italian doctor nine years her junior who'd had a crush on her for *years*—things were looking up! 209 Mulberry Street; 212-334-3097; www.tracyfeith.com

Eres. The prettiest bathing suits and lingerie—of course, it's French. It is (somewhat) expensive, but what the heck—you'll look terrific. They also have sales twice a year. Stores worldwide. www .eresparis.com

Charlotte Moss. Now, we know you can't really have breakfast at Tiffany's (last time we checked, anyway), but if there's a place we would want to camp out overnight, it's here. Oh, and beautiful housewares/gifts, too. 20 East 63rd Street; 212-308-3888; www .charlottemoss.com

Carlyle Hotel. Audrey, Jackie, and Princess Diana all favored this hotel, while Sarah Jessica Parker and her husband, Matthew Broderick, conducted their courtship listening to (the late) Bobby Short . . . how can you go wrong? 35 East 76th Street; 212-744-1600; www.thecarlyle.com

Valentino. AH discovered him early in his career (of course); now he has been discovered by a whole new generation of happening women about town. It does not hurt that he is the nicest gentleman in the world, serves amazing pasta (in the most beautiful surroundings), and loves his dogs, too. 747 Madison Avenue; 212-772-6969. Stores worldwide. www.valentino.com

J. Mendel. That *beyond* mink sweatshirt that you've been coveting? (Originally created for AH by Hubert in 1962. She wore it with black trousers and ballet flats, leaving the set of *Paris When It Sizzles*.) This is the place to get it. 723 Madison Avenue; 212-832-5830. Stores worldwide. www.jmendel.com

Petit Bateau. *The* best T-shirt option (unless you opt for the Hanes white 3-pack). 1094 Madison Avenue; 212-988-8884. Stores worldwide. www.petit-bateau.us

The United Nations. During the UNICEF years, Audrey had lunch at the Members Dining Room on the fourth floor. Befriend a UN worker and have them take you there.

Also stop by and see *Spirit of Audrey*, a beautiful statue commissioned by Rob to commemorate Audrey's life. In front of the James P. Grant Plaza at UNICEF Headquarters. East 44th Street between First and Second avenues. 3 United Nations Plaza.

Council on Foreign Relations. Finally—an organization for all the policy wonks, however stylish, among us. 58 East 68th Street; 212-434-9400. www.cfr.org

The Breakfast at Tiffany's Townhouse. Yes, it is an actual townhouse on the Upper East Side. However, the owner is a friend, and we are not printing the address—just head to 71st Street and start walking east.

Jeffrey Banks. Come *on*, you didn't really expect us to give you the address of one of AH's most stylish (and devoted) friends? Although if we did, you could meet him and end up loving Audrey even more than you already do now.

Physique 57. Of course, AH did not really exercise, but if she did, we think she would probably love Pilates or this modern successor, Physique 57, beloved by dancers, actors, and socialites alike. Located in New York City or Bridgehampton (summer months only). 24 West 57th Street, Suite 805; 212-399-6570; www.physique57.com

Li-Lac Chocolates. Don't get us started about how fabulous this chocolate is. The best. Outstanding. Plus, the fact that Audrey used to get her favorites here (at the former Christopher Street location) makes it even better. And, by the way, she—like Katharine Hepburn—preferred dark chocolate bark. 40 Eighth Avenue at Jane Street, with an outpost in Grand Central Station; www.li-lac chocolates.com

Ralph Lauren. The Mecca of RL-philes (and who isn't?). Audrey and Rob stopped by one time, met Ralph, and everybody became fast friends. 888 Madison Avenue at 72nd Street; 212-434-8000; www.ralphlauren.com

The Bandshell, Central Park. Where Buddy Ebsen and George Peppard have their "heart to heart" talk in *Breakfast at Tiffany's*.

Burger Heaven. Where Audrey enjoyed a hamburger and, later, when she stopped eating red meat, a turkey burger. When she was a model and studying acting before her move to Monaco, Grace Kelly ate here, too. Locations throughout NYC.

Kenneth W. Rendell Gallery. If you are feeling flush, pick up Audrey's letters and commune with greatness. Kenneth W. Rendell Gallery, 989 Madison Avenue at 76th Street; 212-717-1776; www.kwrendell.com

Jason Wu. Who needs *Project Runway*? If we had to pick one up-and-comer following in Hubert's footsteps, our money is on Mr. Wu. This Parsons graduate is young and talented, and respects the past while not being overly beholden to it. www.jasonwustudio.com

| Los Angeles |

The Wagging Tail. AH would have loved this adorable pet shop in Santa Monica. Great for doggy gifts. 1123 Montana Avenue, Santa Monica; 310-656-9663; www.wagwagwag.com

Decades. Frankly, we want to win an Oscar—or get invited to the *Vanity Fair* party—just so we can go here and pick up a dress. Julia

Roberts, Winona Ryder, Nicole Kidman, Liz Goldwyn, and all of the most Audrey gals around are clients. Nice guy Cameron Silver is king of the castle here—and he *really* knows his stuff. Check out his blog while you are at it. 8214½ Melrose; 323-655-0223; www.decadesinc.com

Hamburger Hamlet. A low-key dining spot enjoyed by Audrey, Rob, and Connie Wald. Make sure you split the chocolate dessert. 9201 Sunset Boulevard, West Hollywood; 310-278-4924; www.hamburgerhamlet.com

Williams-Sonoma. Audrey and Hubert shopped here when she visited L.A. Locations nationwide. www.williams-sonoma.com

The Beverly Hills Hotel. For your very Hollywood moment. Skip the Polo Lounge and head to the coffee shop for breakfast. 9641 Sunset Boulevard; 310-276-2251; www.beverlyhillshotel.com

Book Soup. While we don't think AH ever made an appearance here (we know Rob favors Rizzoli in Beverly Hills), "the soup" is our favorite bookstore in L.A. 8818 Sunset Boulevard, West Hollywood; 310-659-3110.

Intersection of Beverly Drive and Santa Monica Boulevard. Drive *carefully* (but stylishly) when you go through this intersection . . . where AH had her fender bender in 1958.

The Chateau Marmont. While AH was doing the family thing down the street at the Beverly Hills Hotel, wild men Bill Holden, Glenn Ford, and Howard Hughes were whooping it up at the chateau.

F. Scott Fitzgerald wrote here (and now favored by current scribes Dominick Dunne, Dana Thomas, and Stephen Gaghan), Jim

Morrison jumped out a window in a moment of drug-fueled exuberance, and Led Zeppelin rode their motorcycles down the hall. After two decades of the hotel's long, slow decline, André Balazs has restored it to its four-star glory days and now cool guys like Johnny Depp, Orlando Bloom, and James de Givenchy en famille stay here during their western jaunts. Frankly, the place can't be all that bad. 8221 Sunset Boulevard, Hollywood; 323-656-1010; www.chateau marmont.com

The Way We Wore. AH bought all of her clothes new, but if she were looking for some Audrey Style vintage clothing, she would ring up Doris Raymond and check out the top quality—and very well documented—things here. Don't miss the second floor. 334 South LaBrea Avenue; 323-937-0870.

JAX. A legendary style emporium that is, sadly, no more. Audrey shopped there, as did practically every star in Hollywood, as well as Audrey Wilder and Connie Wald. They also had an outpost in NYC that Jackie and all of her Kennedy in-laws frequented. Formerly on Wilshire Boulevard in Beverly Hills, catty-corner to the Wilshire Hotel. (RIP)

| London |

65 South Audley Street. Located in the heart of Mayfair, AH and her mother lived here (with the baroness working as a landlady) when they moved to London after the war. Audrey's mother was so conscientious that she could not accompany Audrey on her first trip to America, to star in *Gigi* on Broadway, because she had to stay home and take care of things. There is a pub downstairs. Have a drink and imagine Hepburn's early years.

Bond Street. Where Manolo Blahnik spotted AH catching a cab, in the 1980s. "I saw her, and my heart practically stopped, she was so elegant . . . ," he recalled.

Claridge's Hotel. AH met director William Wyler here testing for *Roman Holiday*. "They were looking for an unknown," she said, "and I was." Brook Street, Mayfair; Claridges.co.uk

Brora. We don't want to say it's the best cashmere in the world—but it's right up there. www.brora.co.uk

| Paris |

Andrea's son Luca says that he "cannot pass a flower shop" without thinking of his mother. Perhaps you will, too.

Walk along the side of the Seine with **Notre Dame** to your right—just like Audrey and Hubert did in the 1970s. Wear your Burberry raincoat and share confidences with a friend.

The top of the stairs at **the Louvre** with the *Winged Victory* in the background. Have your own Audrey/Fred Astaire as Dick Avery channeling Richard Avedon *Funny Face* moment—"Take the picture! Take the picture!"—but, please, don't break your neck.

The Children's Carousel in the Tuileries. Who knows—maybe you will meet your own Cary Grant.

Hotel Raphael. Audrey stayed here, so has Natalie Portman—why not you? 17 Avenue Kléber; www.raphael-hotel.com

Louis Vuitton. Rob bought Audrey a hard-sided makeup case here when they had just begun dating (he noticed that her old one had worn out, and got it for her as a gift)—now *there's* a beau. 38 Avenue de Champs-Elysees; www.louisvuitton.com

Vintage Haute Couture. You can pretend Audrey (or Babe Paley) was your grandmother and left you all this gorgeous stuff after you've seen this shop. Top of the line. Just like our Audrey. Palais Royale.

Poilane Bakery. Founded in 1932, where Hubert still gets his bread. If you visit, ask to go downstairs and see the ovens. Fortunately, they deliver via FedEx to America. 8 rue du Cherche Midi; www.poilane.fr

| Rome |

Greg Peck's Place. Don't think we're not doing our research—we found the apartment where Audrey's character hid out with newspaperman Gregory Peck in *Roman Holiday*. Via Margutta No. 33.

Hassler Hotel. *The* joint in Rome—favored by producers, movie stars, and screenwriters on the studio's dime for decades. Located right on the Spanish Steps, where AH stayed while in Rome. Run by the impeccable (and implacable) Roberto Wirth. As an American, dress properly, keep your voice down, and tip freely. Ask for rooms in the front. www.hotelhasslerroma.com

If you are looking to save a few dollars (which is all relative, of course, in Rome), check out the **International Wine Academy of Rome** (we kid you not), which is next door and Hassler's sister hotel. www.wineacademyroma.com

Excelsior Hotel. Another showstopper. Via Veneto, 125; www.westin.com/excelsiorrome.com

Marisa Padovan. AH had her bespoke bathing suits made here (well, she is not a style icon for nothing). The owner is quoted as saying bikinis cost £400, with a one-piece going for £500. It takes two to three months to have made, but can also be turned around quickly in about a week if you are going on your honeymoon. Located on a side street close to the Spanish Steps. Villa della Carrozze; www.marisapadovan.com

Caffé Greco. Where James Hanson and Gregory Peck hung out playing gin rummy (Greg waiting for his scene, Jimmy waiting for Audrey) during the shooting of *Roman Holiday*. Via Condotti, 84.

| Monte Carlo |

Hotel de Paris. Audrey was filming *Monte Carlo Baby* in 1951 when she was spotted by Colette in the lobby, who said, "Voilà, there is my Gigi!" And a star was born. These days, you have to be a guest of the hotel to enter the lobby, but worth the trip.

| Switzerland |

The ski lift at Megeve, Switzerland. For sharing bon mots with Cary Grant-esque strangers à la *Charade*.

La Paisible. We're not suggesting you take the forty-minute train ride from Geneva to visit AH's former 1740-era home (surrounded by a fieldstone wall). We are just saying that if you do, take a left at the train station and walk about fifteen minutes to the very quiet (albeit pretty) country village . . . where there is absolutely nothing going on. Just the way Audrey liked it.

There used to be a two-room Audrey museum, put together as an homage by her neighbors, which was closed after Sean and Luca took their mother's things back (after a five-year loan). "This is my mother's resting place," groused Sean, "not Graceland." Route de Bière, Tolochenaz.

| Ireland |

Shelbourne Hotel. Audrey met her father here in 1964 after a nearly twenty-year absence. 27 St. Stephen's Green, Dublin.

MISCELLANEOUS

Unicefusa.org

International Campaign for Tibet (ICT). The Dalai Lama's lifelong mission. With people like Richard Gere, Kerry Kennedy, and Melissa Mathison, the screenwriter for *E.T.*, on the board of directors, you know Audrey would have been involved. www.savetibet.org

The Audrey rose. Spring Hill Nurseries created the Audrey rose in Hepburn's honor. Now it seems to have been discontinued. Perhaps Audrey Fans can start a petition to have it reinstated. When Audrey learned that a rose had been named for her, she said, "Oh, this is the *most* romantic thing!" We agree. www.springhillnursery.com

WOULD AUDREY . . .

Have sold her letters? Absolutely not. In 2003, Fidelma Hepburn-Ruston, the third wife of Audrey's father, put twenty-six of Audrey's letters up for sale with Kenneth W. Rendell, a specialist in autographs, historical letters, documents, manuscripts, and rare books, and boy, does this annoy Audrey's sons and Rob. We think AH would have been appalled.

For the record, Rob has beautiful letters from Audrey that will never see the light of day. Instead, he intends to leave them to Sean and Luca.

Have sat for an interview with Oprah Winfrey? Possibly. Although neither Jacqueline Kennedy Onassis, Princess Grace of Monaco, nor Princess Diana ever made the pilgrimage to Chicago, there is only one reason Audrey might have, *might* have agreed to an interview—to promote the work of UNICEF.

Although AH hated sitting for televised interviews, and half joked about the tough line of questioning Phil Donohue followed when he asked her about her weight, her age, and plastic surgery during the first minute and a half of his interview with her ("and they told me you were so nice," she half seriously chided him), she might have made an exception for Miss O.

In addition to Africa, having zero interest in getting married, and their love of dogs, pasta, and books, they also could have bonded over their shared love of All Things Valentino.

And we know it would have had the highest ratings of any Oprah show. *Ever.*

Believe in the talismanic power of clothing? Yes. Audrey was always nervous about speaking in public or giving speeches on behalf of UNICEF. But she confided to Givenchy, "When I talk about

UNICEF in front of the television cameras, I am naturally emotional. Wearing your blouses makes me feel protected."

Stay grounded? Yes. As Rob observes, "In her personal life, there was a lot of pain. We talked about it to some extent because we lived through the same war, and the same deprivation, and I think when you are exposed to that kind of strife and deprivation, you are grateful for anything good that comes afterwards, but in Audrey, fame, when it came so early in life, it didn't go to her head. She remained very realistic. So she knew that every individual had to suffer adversity, so she never said, 'Why me?' "

Remain cautiously optimistic? Yes. In general, Audrey tended to look at the more positive aspect of a situation. Once, asked if there was a downside to being a movie star, she replied, "It was never a burden, and there really isn't a downside. Like in anything, you can find a problem. I think there was when my second son was born, and I was at that time living in Rome, and I could not take him anywhere—not to a park, not down the street, not put him on a terrace without paparazzi. That again was very difficult because it wasn't me bothering the child, but to have photographers jumping out from behind trees, and he'd be howling because he was so startled! But then again, a dear friend who had a little garden in Rome, told me: 'Bring your child here, with other children, as often as you want, I'd love to have them in the garden, it would make me happy!'

"So there are the little difficult moments . . . I can think of no downside."

Look dated? No. Fashion historian June Weir noted that "Grace Kelly looks dated, but not Audrey. In terms of fashion and style, she was so far ahead in the way that she thought of herself. Even at the very end, she looked twenty years younger."

From a man's perspective, Rob thought it was her vivaciousness that made Audrey so au courant. "They talk about the things that Audrey wore, but I think it was the person inside. When she wore her evening clothes, she was almost like a child dressing up. Because most of the times she wore jeans and a Lacoste shirt, it was a kick for her. But I really do think it's the woman inside the clothes. I think it's one of the reasons people try to look like Audrey, because they think if they wore those clothes, they would seem to have the same energy or be the same person.

"Apart from that, she didn't follow fashion. She continued to wear what suited her, and it was nothing uncomfortable or extravagant. Grace Kelly is a classic beauty, but you almost think of her as a beautiful painting, as two dimensional. But Audrey remains alive."

Move beyond her fear?

Yes. Contrary to how easy she made it look, Rob felt that "acting didn't come easy to Audrey at all. She was as nervous with her last picture, *Always*, as she was with *Roman Holiday*." Sean once commented that "she was scared, man, scared."

Look at the big picture?

Yes. Geopolitics and couture aside, Audrey was about one thing: peace. Having experienced the brutal ravages of war firsthand, and through her work with UNICEF, she knew the intolerable cost of conflict. She was not naive about the ways of the world, once asking a group of U.S. senators, "We study war. Why can't we study and have a science of peace?"

Let it go?

Yes. On the eve of World War II, her father left Audrey and her mother at the mercy of the German army. "Don't discount anything awful you hear or read about the Nazis," she once said. "It's worse than you could ever imagine." Both her husbands cheated on her. Still, she kept her heart open to the possibility of human kindness and redemption.

Phone it in? Never. Not as an actress. Not for UNICEF, and not for her friends.

Talk about herself? "As a child," said Audrey, "I was taught that it was bad manners to bring attention to yourself, and to never, ever make a spectacle of yourself." Now if only more non-Tony/Oscar-winning people would follow her lead.

Look back? No. "I *loathe* nostalgia!" said Diana Vreeland, and so did Audrey. Once she left Hollywood, that was it.

Put others first? Yes. Audrey realized that fame and even beauty is short-lived. And according to Rob, "She consciously decided to remain herself. So the focus was less on herself than on the boys and on family and her loved ones." Several weeks before she died, Rob stayed with her in the hospital in New York City. He slept on a cot in her room and in the morning when he got up, she noticed he had not slept well, and when he was out showering, she asked one of the nurses if they could bring a foam mattress pad for the cot, so that he would be more comfortable. Years later, thinking of this, Rob found it so touching, because she was in so much pain herself and yet she was thinking of him, in even the smallest ways.

Be as cool as she seemed? Actually, she was probably cooler. Kevin Aucoin knew that "certain people have a public image, and their private self are two totally different things — miles apart! And she was her public image. And that would shock most people, because her pubic persona was so amazing that you couldn't imagine that anyone could actually be like that!"

And we are still picking up pointers from her. As Vera Wang put it: "The world came around to her style, she did not ever come around to the world's style."

Be remembered? You tell us.

Among her friends, John Isaac says that "sometimes even now, when I am in some kind of trouble, I think of her." Bob Willoughby admits that he "prays for her every day." Jeffrey Banks happened to be in the Ralph Lauren store on 72nd Street shortly after Audrey died. "Moon River" came over the sound system. Jeffrey was so upset at hearing her voice that he walked out.

Julie Leifermann said, "When she touched your life, it's something that you don't easily forget. She had that ability with people in her life—to affect you in ways that were very personal. That's just the kind of person she was. That had nothing to do with the movie star.

"I think, overall, she was the kind of person that we all would aspire to be. The human being. And, unfortunately, you don't meet many people like that. And I think that's the personal gift to us—her ability to grace us with being herself."

"Most women of style are courageous."–Vera Wang

To continue Audrey's work,
please consider supporting UNICEF.

www.unicefusa.org

Acknowledgments

I would like to thank the friends, fans, and fellow biographers of Audrey's who were so generous with their time and insight. Without their contributions, there would not be a book. I first became acquainted with Audrey's world with my first book, *Audrey Style*, and it has been a privileged journey ever since.

Many people spoke to me out of their friendship and respect for Audrey, and for that I would like to thank Liz Aiello, the late Kevin Aucoin, Letitia Baldrige, Jeffrey Banks, Jeffrey Bilhuber, Janis Blackschlager, the late Rosemary Clooney, Colin Cowie, Stuart Crowner, Darac, Dale DeGroff, Tiffany Dubin, Dominick Dunne, Tzetzi Ganev, Bobi Garland, Garren, Hubert de Givenchy, James de Givenchy, William A. Henry III, Mellody Hobson, John Isaac, Richard Johnson, James Katz, David Kirsch, Michael Kors, Ralph Lauren, Kevin Mazur, Steven Meisel, Polly Mellon, Beth Mendelson, Ellen Mirojnick, Joseph Montebello, Cathy O'Brien, the late Gregory Peck, Candy Pratts Price, Doris Raymond, Amanda Ross, Jane Ross, Cynthia Rowley, Liz Santelli, Cameron Silver, Dr. Devendra Singh, Andy Spade, Steven Spielberg, Christy Turlington, Connie Wald, Vera Wang, June Weir, Audrey Wilder, Bob Willoughby, Robert Wolders, Jason Wu.

Audrey Hepburn is one of the most well documented women of our time. I would like to recognize the journalists and biographers who came before me—Cecil Beaton, Marie Brenner, Professor Richard Brown, David Chierichetti, Amy Fine Collins, Stanley Donen, Dominick Dunne, Marc Eliot, Charles Higham, Hedda Hopper, Larry King, Barry Paris, J. D. Podolsky, Stephen M. Silverman, Annette Tapert, Dana Thomas, Gore Vidal, Alexander Walker, Barbara Walters, and Ian Woodward.

One of my favorite parts of writing is the research. In addition to all of the people that I interviewed, I would also like to thank Faye Thompson, who oversees the stunning AMPAS library in Los Angeles—which is inspiring enough to make anyone want to work in the movie business—and Barbara Hall, who was such a great help to me as I researched AH, Cecil Beaton, Hedda Hopper, and the directors she worked with.

Any serious style biographer must also recognize the Aladdin's Cave that is the Condé Nast library—I would practically move in there if I could. It is a veritable treasure trove of all things *Vogue*. Cynthia Cathcart, again, was of tremendous assistance.

My Los Angeles research assistant, Lorrie Ivas, is a great friend and a very insightful commentator on popular style. I would also like to recognize Justin Luft, the Computer Guy who keeps my life running—no small thing to a writer these days.

Linda Chester is not only my agent, she is also a friend, advisor, and inspiration who has made many of my dreams come true. I feel extremely grateful to have her in my life. Gary Jaffe of the Linda Chester Agency is also a tremendous ally, and one of the funniest men I know.

Without a publishing house, a writer is just someone sitting around Starbucks with a laptop and a dream. Working with Gotham Books has been a joy. In addition to publisher William Shinker, I would like to thank my editor, Lauren Marino, and her more than able assistant editor, Brianne Ramagosa, for making *WWAD?* such a positive experience. I look forward to further collaborations. Illustrator Monika Roe brought our Audrey-inspired sketches beautifully to life. Paula Reedy gave the manuscript a close reading, while Sabrina Bowers was an exceptional design manager. And managing editor Susan Schwartz and associate production editor Katie Cicatelli made sure this book actually made it to the printer on time.

Finally, I know that I am extremely fortunate to have met so many of Audrey's friends and fans over the past decade. I would like to dedicate this book to her fans around the world who keep her memory, and her good works, alive. Thank you.

Index

accessories, 141
age, 143
air travel, 116–25, 129
alone time, 81–82, 128
Always, 214
anger, 84
animals, 70, 81, 110, 113, 174, 215
Anne Fontaine, 140
appetite and food choices, 104–7,
    108, 117, 122, 162
Aucoin, Kevin, 67, 218–19
auctioning of *Breakfast at Tiffany's*
    dress, 149, 150–51
audience authority, 68
autographs, 31–32

Banana Republic, 140
Banks, Jeffrey, 41, 161, 192, 197, 248
bathing, 175
Beaton, Cecil
    on Audrey imitators, 146–47

initial impression of Audrey,
    48–49, 51
and *My Fair Lady*, 110, 201
on personality of Audrey, 108
on shoes of Audrey, 134
beauty, sources of, 68, 82, 108,
    160–61, 162
Bilhuber, Jeffrey, 2, 88, 89,
    100–101
birthday of Audrey, 14, 226–29
Bisset, Jacqueline, 32
Blackschlager, Janis, 31–32, 85, 98
body shapes, 63–64
Bogdanovich, Peter, 209
Bose headphones, 121
Breakfast at Tiffany's, 149–51, 183,
    199–200, 227–28
Broadway, Florida, 106
brows, 137
Brynner, Doris, 93, 107
Brynner, Victoria, 93–94
Bush, George H. W., 102

cameras, looking great for, 30–31
candles, 95
Cartier, 142
cashmere wraps, 122
celebrities with Audrey style, 196–98
celebrity, 3–4, 62
Chanel, Coco, 141, 148, 151, 158
Charade, 55, 200–201
charisma, 41–42
charm, 28
children
    Audrey's love of, 70, 81, 90, 113,
      210
    and marriages of Audrey, 47, 48,
      170, 189, 191
    as priority for Audrey, 43
    See also Dotti, Luca; Ferrer, Sean
china, 95–96
chocolate, 107, 215, 229
Clooney, Rosemary, 56–57
clothing styles and choices
    auction for *Breakfast at Tiffany's*
      dress, 149, 150–51
    cashmere wraps, 122
    casual clothing, 218
    and confidence, 143, 244–45
    consistency in, 220
    and cultivating a style, 133–34
    and film costumes, 144–47, 149,
      150–51, 187, 209–10
    Givenchy's influence on, 144–48
    importance of, 24
    influence of Audrey on, 2
    and knockoffs, 161
    and labels, 161, 162
    the little black dress, 148–51
    preferences in, 230
    and tailoring, 141, 160
    trying on, 163
    while traveling, 120–21
    white shirts, 138–41
Collins, Judy, 195

colors, favorite, 110, 215, 230
commercials, 200
compassion, 3–4
complaining, 226
contracts, 23, 198
correspondence, 102–4, 228, 244
Council on Foreign Relations,
    207–8
Cowie, Colin, 103
Crane's stationary, 104
Crazy Horse burlesque show, 217
Crowner, Stu, 84, 202
crying, 175
Cukor, George, 75, 182, 201
cultural influence of Audrey, 2–3

Dalai Lama, 225, 230
dancing, 15–16, 17, 72, 153, 166–67
dating, 37–45, 51–54, 60, 64–65.
    See also love and romantic
    relationships
death of Audrey, 223–26
decorators, home, 109–10
De Rossi, Alberto, 135
De Rossi, Grazia, 135
Dickinson, Thorold, 14
diet/exercise regime, 107–8, 151–54,
    155–56, 216
dignity, 207, 211, 224
disappearing from public life,
    26–27, 54, 83
disappointment, dealing with, 74–78
discipline, 152–53
discretion, 27, 40–41, 65, 160
dogs, 110, 113, 174, 215
Donen, Stanley
    and *Charade*, 201
    on film career of Audrey, 193
    on Finney and Audrey, 189
    friendship of, 77, 202
    on multilingualism of Audrey, 143

and *Two for the Road*, 32, 185–86, 187–88
on work ethic of Audrey, 202
Donohue, Phil, 15, 244
Dotti, Andrea
    early relationship with, 65
    engagement to, 45, 142
    and in-laws of Audrey, 92–93
    marriage to, 24, 91, 170, 171
    post-marriage relationship with, 212–13
Dotti, Luca, 3, 91, 208, 213
driving, 111–12
Dunne, Dominick
    on Audrey's dogs, 100
    on enthusiasm of Audrey, 60
    on Ferrer, 48, 71
    on in-laws of Audrey, 92
    on relationships of Audrey, 5
    on telephone habits of Audrey, 33

eating. *See* food and eating habits
Edwards, Blake, 223
ego, 71–72, 92, 218
employment, 54, 61. *See also* film career
enigmatic reputation of Audrey, 27, 60
enthusiasm, 60
Eternal Girlfriend trap, 58
Eula, Joe, 143
exercise. *See* diet/exercise regime
eye makeup, 136–37

faith, 60–61, 174, 246
family
    and alone time, 128
    and hard times, 175
    and home, 109
    importance of, 87, 208, 215, 220

relationships within, 89–94
    See also specific people
Famous, Audrey's dog, 99–100, 142
fans, 31–32, 208–9
father of Audrey. *See* Hepburn-Ruston, Joseph
fears, 23, 190, 246
Ferrer, José, 56–57
Ferrer, Mel
    on *Breakfast at Tiffany's*, 183
    Clooney on, 56–57
    divorce, 91, 191, 212
    and driving accident, 111–12
    early relationship with, 37, 42–43, 45, 54
    ego of, 71
    film appearance of, 210
    on Frings, 23
    and *Green Mansions*, 167–70
    marriage to, 92, 183–84, 201
    and parents of Audrey, 90, 177
    personality of, 49
    post-marriage relationship with, 47–48
Ferrer, Sean
    on Audrey's love life, 178
    birth of, 91
    childhood of, 208
    and correspondence of Audrey, 228, 244
    and death of Audrey, 224, 225
    on Dotti, 171
    and Gap ad, 3
    and parents' marriage, 47, 48, 189, 191
    and photographers, 111
    and photo-memoir of Audrey, 221
    and real estate, 200
figure, 16, 63–64, 107–8, 151
film career, 11–34
    and contracts, 23, 198
    early years of, 17–19

film career (*cont'd*)
  less successful films of, 200
  and salary of Audrey, 198
  and star-quality of Audrey, 2,
    19–21
  years prior to, 12–14
  See also specific films
film costumes, 144–47, 149, 150–51,
  187, 209–10
finances
  financial independence, 54, 195
  Hobson's guidelines for, 194–96
  and personal responsibility, 200
  and real estate, 53, 200
  and salary of Audrey, 198
Finney, Albert, 32, 187, 189, 190
flirting, 52
flowers in the home, 94, 95, 97, 101,
  109, 110
Fontaine, Anne, 140
food and eating habits, 104–7, 108,
  117, 122, 162
forgiveness, 160, 176–77
Fraker, Bud, 18
friendships
  the AH Rules for, 52
  boundaries in, 77
  and hard times, 174, 178
  loyalty to, 202
  as priority for Audrey, 46, 69, 208
  See also specific individuals
Frings, Kurt, 23, 194, 202
furniture, 101, 110

Gallagher, Mary, 37
Galliano, John, 150
Ganev, Tzetzi, 22–23
Gap, 2–3, 140
gardens, 88
Gaulle, Charles de, 80
Gazzara, Ben, 172, 210

generosity of spirit, 73, 84–85, 160,
  202, 247
gifts, 44–45, 92–93
Givenchy, Hubert de
  and Audrey's dresses, 149
  clothing designs of, 24, 244–45
  and death of Audrey, 225
  on discretion of Audrey, 41
  and film costumes, 144–47, 149,
    150–51
  friendship of, 4, 128, 147–48, 202,
    215
  and Jackie Kennedy Onassis, 158
  and jewelry, 142
  and perfume, 203
  and rosebushes, 94
Givenchy, James de, 142
grace, 32, 150, 211
Grant, Cary, 55
gratitude, 177–78, 191, 193
green lifestyle, 107, 113
Green Mansions, 167–70
grooming, 134–35

Hanson, James
  business advice of, 65
  and Ella van Heemstra, 90
  engagement to, 37, 40, 45–46,
    47, 57
hardship, 165–79
  and commitment, 167–70
  dealing with, 166–67, 171–72,
    226–27
  moving beyond, 173–74, 176
  and tenacity, 170
Harris, Radie, 43
Harrison, Rex, 26
Head, Edith, 18, 107, 141, 145
healthy living, 104–8. *See also*
  diet/exercise regime; food and
  eating habits

Heemstra, Ella van
    aspirations of, 14–15
    lessons from, 84
    relationship with, 89–90, 128,
        175, 215
    on talent of Audrey, 73–74
    walking pace of, 108
Hepburn, Katharine, 5, 33–34, 35,
    49, 140, 153
Hepburn-Ruston, Fidelma, 244
Hepburn-Ruston, Joseph, 15, 90,
    177, 229
hip-to-waist ratio, 63–64
hobbies, 113
Hobson, Mellody, 194–96
Holden, William
    on popularity of Audrey, 226
    relationship of Audrey with, 37,
        42, 43, 47, 57, 184, 213
    travel of, 59, 116–17
home style, 87–113
    the AH Checklist for, 95–96
    decorating style, 88, 100–101,
        109
    healthy living, 104–8
    and ironing, 98–99
    and personal letters, 102–4
    and pets, 99–100
    and table settings, 96–97
Hopper, Hedda
    on acting lessons, 201
    on character preparation, 17
    on contracts, 23
    on early years, 12
    on figure, 104, 132
    on Times cover, 177–78
humility, 70–71
humor, 76, 206

in-law, Audrey as, 92–93
instincts, 187, 201, 220

integrity, 72, 108
intelligence, 143
interests, cultivation of, 72
Internet, 65, 112
interviews, 24–25, 28, 244
introspection, 75–76
iPods, 122, 127
ironing, 98–99, 127
Isaac, John, 72, 206–7, 217, 224,
    248

jewelry, 142
Johanssen, Aud, 13
John Paul II, 219
Johnson, Richard, 25
Jong, Leendert de, 129
Joujon-Roche, Gregory, 156
The Juicing Bible (Crocker and
    Eagles), 155

Kate Spade stationary, 104
Kate's Paperie stationary, 104
Kennedy, John F., 37, 42, 57,
    158–59
Keys, Wendy, 23, 169
Kilgallen, Dorothy, 59
King, Larry, 70, 219
King, Martin Luther, Jr., 205
Kirsch, David, 155–56
Kors, Michael, 144, 192

La Paisible, 53, 87–88, 94
Lauren, Ralph, 23, 124, 192
Lazar, Irving "Swifty," 220–21
Lebowitz, Fran, 133
legacy of Audrey, 226
Leifermann, Julie, 106, 248
letters, personal, 102–4, 228, 244
life lessons of Audrey, 226–29

Lincoln Center Film Society Award, 218
lips and lip color, 137
the little black dress, 148–51
Loos, Anita, 46, 49
love and romantic relationships, 37–65
   Audrey's need for, 38, 68–69
   dating, 37–45, 51–54, 60, 64–65
   and Eternal Girlfriend trap, 58–59
   guidelines for, 51–54, 61–62
   and hardships, 5–6, 178
   importance of, 160
   leaving, 45–48
   love-at-first-sight, 65
   mistakes in, 171–72
   See also marriage; Wolders, Robert
low-key persona, 32, 73, 92, 218
loyalty, 167–70, 202
luggage, 118, 120

makeup, 4, 88, 119, 135–37, 160, 162, 163
manicures/pedicures, 117, 163
manners, 91
marriage
   the AH Rules for, 51–52
   and Audrey as spouse, 92
   commitment to, 45
   marriages of Audrey, 57, 170, 171, 178, 212–13
   and money, 195
   as priority for Audrey, 43
   See also Dotti, Andrea; Ferrer, Mel; Wolders, Robert
mascara, 136, 160, 163
massage, 162, 175
materialism, 44–45
Mazur, Kevin, 30–31

Mealand, Richard, 14
media, 24–25, 27–30, 79, 80
meditation, 174
Mele, Dreda, 146, 148
Mellon, Polly, 145
metabolism, 107, 152
miscarriages, 91, 191
Miss Golightly's Champagne Passion recipe, 228
modesty, 20, 132, 134
Moss, Charlotte, 109
mother. *See* Heemstra, Ella van
motherhood, 90–91, 92, 111, 170.
   See also Dotti, Luca; Ferrer, Sean
movie star career. *See* film career
Mrs. John L. Strong stationary, 104
multitasking, 83
music, 72, 95, 109, 230
My Fair Lady, 26, 74–75, 201

napping, 111, 215
Nazis, 15, 16, 246
Nesbitt, Cathleen, 68
New York City, 210
New York Post's Page Six, 25
nicknames, 229
nostalgia, 176, 216, 247
The Nun's Story, 231

O'Keeffe, Georgia, 124
Oliver!, 182
Onassis, Jacqueline Kennedy
   Audrey compared to, 157–59
   and Audrey's autobiography, 221
   and exercise, 153
   and gifts, 44–45
   and home decorators, 109–10
   and telephone calls, 83
opinions, expressing, 199–200

organic food, 106–7
Oscar awards, 74–75
O'Toole, Peter, 229
outlook, 231, 245

packing, 115, 118–20
Paley, Babe, 102, 153
parents. See Heemstra, Ella van;
    Hepburn-Ruston, Joseph
Paris, Barry, 169
Paris When It Sizzles, 149
peace, 220, 246
Peck, Gregory, 1, 6, 42, 60, 85, 214
Petit Bateau, 140
pets, 99–100, 110, 174
Pfeiffer, Michelle, 156
photographs, looking great in, 30–31
poetry, 72, 206–7, 230
point of view (POV), 133
political life, 219, 231
Portman, Natalie, 196
posture, 138, 160
practicality, 129, 245
pregnancies, 154
Presley, Elvis, 126
press and media, 24–25, 27–30, 79,
    80
Previn, André, 26, 201
Price, Candy Pratts, 134–35, 150,
    152, 192, 219
private life, 26–27, 60, 76, 87, 219
professionalism, 201
publicity and publicists, 24–25, 26,
    203

reading, 122
real estate, 53, 200. See also La
    Paisible
religion, 84
Rendlesham, Lady Claire, 187

respect, 53, 59, 76
responsibility, 22–23, 194, 219
Roberts, Julia, 219
Rogers, Henry, 203
Roman Holiday, 1, 13–14, 21
Rowley, Cynthia, 134, 163, 220
Rufino, Robert, 96–97

Sabrina, 144–45, 149
"saint" references, 220
salary, 198
scotch, 215, 227, 231
self-perception, 5, 132
sensitivity, 207
70% waist-to-hip ratio, 63–64
shoes, 121, 134, 138, 229
shopping, 112, 178, 231, 233–43
Singh, Devendra, 63, 64
sleep, 111, 162, 215
smiling, 160
smoking, 152, 153–54, 155, 215
Smythson stationary, 104
Spade, Andy, 192
Spielberg, Steven, 214
spouse, Audrey as, 92
stage fright, 23, 246
star-quality, 2, 19–21
stationery, 102, 104
stress, 80, 154
style, 131–63
    and Audrey-esque celebrities,
        196–98
    diet/exercise regime, 151–56
    essentials of, 160
    and Givenchy, 144–51
    guidelines for, 133–44
    at home, 89
    of Jackie Kennedy Onassis,
        157–59
    and money, 94
    and self-perception of Audrey, 132

style (*cont'd*)
    Wang on, 247
    See also clothing styles and
        choices
success, 70–74, 183–84
swimming, 111

table settings, 96–97
Taffin, 142
Tagore, Rabindranath, 206–7, 230
tailors, 141, 160
telephone calls, 33, 83, 84
tenacity, 170, 179
They All Laughed, 209–10
Thomas Pink, 140
Tiffany's, 142
tipping, 120
travel, 115–29
    hotels, 125–27
    in-flight priorities, 120–25
    packing, 115, 118–20
    preflight preparations, 117–18,
        120
    souvenirs from, 101
Turlington, Christy, 149–50, 154
Two for the Road, 116, 185–91,
        231

unforgettable nature of Audrey,
    19–20, 41, 69, 248
UNICEF (United Nations
    Children's Fund)
    devotion of Audrey to, 3, 205–8,
        215
    donations to, 161, 227
    fund-raising for, 218
    humanitarian trips of, 4, 205,
        223
    and Wolders, 205, 206, 207, 220,
        223, 224

Valentino, 141, 150
Van Cleef & Arpels, 142
vision, importance of having, 24
voice, 138, 160
Vreeland, Diana, 116, 176, 247
vulnerability, 68

waist-to-hip ratio, 63–64
Wald, Connie, 106, 162, 181, 194,
    228
walking, 153
Walters, Barbara, 29, 212
Wang, Vera, 157, 247
Warner, Jack, 74, 75
weight, 16, 104, 107
Weir, June, 245
white shirts, 138–41
wife, Audrey as, 92
Wilde, Oscar, 135
Wilder, Audrey, 5, 99, 147, 184, 191,
    231
Wilder, Billy, 17, 69, 184, 202
Willoughby, Bob
    on beauty of Audrey, 82
    on discretion of Audrey, 65
    on Famous, 99
    on Ferrer, 48
    and *Green Mansions*, 167–68, 169
    on Holden, 213
    initial meeting with Audrey,
        17–19
    on legs of Audrey, 231
    on loss of Audrey, 248
    on motherhood of Audrey, 111
    on *My Fair Lady* set, 201
    on relationships of Audrey, 42, 77
    on respect for Audrey, 76
Winfrey, Oprah, 212, 244
Winston, Harry, 142
Wolders, Robert
    on anger of Audrey, 84

on celebrity of Audrey, 3
and correspondence of Audrey,
        228, 244
on death of Audrey, 224–25
described, 177
on Ella van Heemstra, 89
on fears of Audrey, 190
on Ferrer, 184
gifts from Audrey, 71
Johnson on, 25
on nostalgia of Audrey, 176
partnership with Audrey, 62,
        173–74, 178–79, 210, 211,
        212, 215
on personality of Audrey, 75–76
and pets, 100
on political life of Audrey, 231
on practicality of Audrey, 6–7,
        245
on relationships of Audrey, 70
on self-perception of Audrey, 5,
        132

on Spielberg, 214
on status of Audrey, 4
on style of Audrey, 245–46
and UNICEF work, 205, 206,
        207, 220, 223, 224
on values of Audrey, 20
on work ethic of Audrey, 181
Wolf, Henry, 217
work ethic, 13, 181, 202
Wyler, William, 12, 13–14, 21, 202

youthful appearance, 108

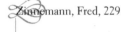Zinnemann, Fred, 229

| About the Author |

Pamela Keogh is the author of *Audrey Style, Jackie Style,* and *Elvis Presley: The Man. The Life. The Legend.* Her work has been featured on the *Today* show, *Larry King Live, Vanity Fair, The New York Times, Town & Country, InStyle, People* magazine, *Harper's Bazaar, Entertainment Tonight,* the *Los Angeles Times,* the BBC, and hundreds of other media outlets around the world.

A graduate of Vassar College, she lives in New York City. Her Web site is www.pamelakeogh.com.